Grant Andrews & Ma

How to Understand and Accept

Your Gay Son

Grant Andrews

Malan van der Walt

How to Understand and Accept Your Gay Son

Copyright © 2015 by Grant Andrews and Malan van der Walt

All rights reserved. No part of this publication may be reproduced, distributed, or transmitted in any form or by any means, including photocopying, recording, or other electronic or mechanical methods, without the prior written permission of the authors, except in the case of brief quotations embodied in critical reviews and certain other noncommercial uses permitted by copyright law. For permission requests, write to the authors at the address below.

Inspired Living Books
29 Postnet Suite
PO Box X04
Kuils River
Cape Town
South Africa
7479

The advice and information contained in this book are intended to supplement, and not replace, consultation with a trained mental health professional. Every effort has been made to ensure the accuracy of the information contained herein and the effectiveness of any advice given. The authors do not assume and hereby disclaim any liability to any party for any loss, damage or disruption caused by errors or omissions, or as a result of any information or advice contained in this book.

Grant Andrews & Malan van der Walt

Cover design by Pro_Ebookcovers
Edited by Anthea Carmeline
Edited by Kenneth Hopson

Twitter: @gandrewslife
Email: grant.andrews@backtoincomplete.com
malanvdw@gmail.com

Inspired Living Books

www.inspiredlivingbooks.com

Acknowledgements

The authors would like to thank Carmelita Mack, Katrina du Toit, Kiki Kargaard and Franchureen Baartman for their willingness to read and comment on early drafts of this book.

We are indebted to our editors, Kenneth Hopson and Anthea Carmeline, for their tireless work.

Thank you to our parents for their support and for making it possible for us to be the men we are today.

A special thanks to the LGBT students and young people who we have the privilege of working with. Your bravery, resilience and determination to work towards a better world is part of what inspired us to write this book.

Grant Andrews & Malan van der Walt

Table of Contents

Foreword 9

UNDERSTANDING YOUR GAY SON 11
Introduction 11
What this book offers you 14
How to use this book 15

Chapter 1: So Where Do I Start? 17
What is the acronym LGBT? 17
What is homosexuality? And what is it NOT? 19
It is NOT: 20
Are there any signs that I can look out for to see whether my son might be gay? 21

Chapter 2: Why is my son gay? 23
Is it a birth defect? 24
Did I do something wrong as a parent? 24
Is it because his father was absent? Is it because he is too close to his mother? 25
Is there anything I can do now to change him? 26
What about those "ex-gay" people I have been hearing about? .. 27
Is it a choice to be gay? 29
What are the biological reasons for my son being gay? 32
What do the experts say about being gay? 33
How your son's mental health is affected 34

Chapter 3: Homophobia: The deadly threat to your son's mental health 38
What is homophobia? 38
1. Homophobia as expressed by the fear of gay sex 39

    2. Homophobia as expressed by the fear of femininity in men 42
    3. Homophobia due to fear that gay men will hit on straight men 44
    4. Homophobia due to the fear of HIV 46
    Internalized homophobia 49
    How can I protect my child from homophobia? 52

Chapter 4: What does God say? 54
    Why does the Bible seem to condemn homosexuality? 54
    Did all cultures and all religions always hate LGBT people? 57
    What does the Bible really say? 59
    It seems pretty clear that the God hates gay people, right? 61
    What are the other interpretations of the way the Bible "condemns" homosexuality? 64
    So where does that leave me and my faith? 72

Chapter 5: Gay culture: why does my son love Lady Gaga so much? 75
    Is there such a thing as "gay culture"? 75
    Why do people often refer to the "gay community"? 77
    Gay culture as a subculture 78
    Gay culture as a counterculture 79
    Gay people as surrogate families 81
    Gay Pride 83
    Gay spaces 84
    Gay relationships and dating 85
    Being in the closet 88
    Coming out 89

Chapter 6: I'm not supposed to ask this, but... 92
    Are gay people destined for a lonely, sad life? 92
    Do older gay men recruit younger children to be gay? 93
    Is being gay equivalent to or related to pedophilia? 94
    But they can't have kids! Doesn't that make it unnatural? 95

Are there "men" and "women" in gay relationships, and which role does my son take? 97
Is it okay to wonder about or ask about who is the "top" or the "bottom" in my son's relationship? 98
But gay men aren't real men, are they? 99
Will a child be at a disadvantage by having two same-sex parents? 101

ACCEPTING YOUR GAY SON 103

With some useful scripts to use for those challenging conversations 103
I don't think I can ever accept my son, and it makes me feel terrible that our relationship is so damaged. 103
I've done the work and soul-searching, and I'm ready to accept my son. Now what? 105
I think that my son is gay but he hasn't spoken to me about it. What should I do? 105
My son just caught me off guard and told me he is gay! How do I react? 110
I feel uncomfortable with the thought of my son being with another guy. How do I overcome this discomfort? 113
What NOT to say to your son when you find out he is gay 120
I've already said some of these damaging things. What now? ... 126
Is my son really the same person? He seems so different to me. 127
How do I talk to my son about sex and the risk of HIV? 128
I would like my son to abstain from sex. Should I tell him this? 131
I'm worried about what people will say about my son or about me. 132
How can I help combat homophobia in my community? 133
What if my partner or co-parent does not accept my son, but I do? 135

How to Understand and Accept Your Gay Son

I won't have any grandchildren. This makes me really sad and disappointed. 136

I feel more settled in my new identity as the parent of a gay son. But I am not sure how to tell important people in my life about this. 138

Are there any additional resources which I can use to aid me in my journey of accepting my gay son? 140

Advocacy groups and informational sites 140

Representations of Gay Men 141

Glossary 147

About the authors 149

Grant Andrews & Malan van der Walt

Foreword

I was crushed to hear that my son is gay, even though I had thought he might be. My husband was broken and distraught. He had absolutely no clue that our son is gay.

Our highly intelligent son, our wonderful child who has so much understanding and insight into the emotional pain of others, who has the best answers to help heal the emotional obstacles of others – how can he be gay?

It is a long and difficult road to walk.

A lonely road.

It is filled with struggles. It seemed abhorrent to me. Daily snide comments made about gays make life as the parents of a gay child lonely and marginalized.

Until I came to the realization – with much patience and love for my gay child – that he is a whole person, even if he is gay.

That is as simple as it is.

Today I have respect for him; he has walked a long and lonely road for many years.

A road that is longer than what a parent can even imagine. Being reproached and taunted. Mockery is an everyday reality faced by gay young people. It doesn't change much by the time they reach adulthood.

How to Understand and Accept Your Gay Son

No one chooses this path. It is only the brave ones who make peace with it through a lot of introspection, struggle and self-acceptance.

I have complete and total peace. My gay child is one of my four children whom I love exactly the same. It enriched my life when I could take myself out of my safe comfort zone and accept him. But it wasn't easy.

My gay son is my child with his own personality. Someone whom I admire for what he is and for what he has achieved.

Just like his two sisters and his brother.

I thank God in His grace for bringing me to this point. And I thank Him for the peace in my heart.

I thank Him also for allowing our child to take us into his confidence and for having him trust us until we understood and accepted him.

He is a whole person with someone from his own gender. Just like a heterosexual person is complete with someone from the opposite sex.

Leonore van der Walt
Mother of Malan van der Walt

Grant Andrews & Malan van der Walt

Understanding Your Gay Son

Introduction

We are happy that you picked up this book. It shows that you are committed to embark on a journey with your son and loved ones towards understanding and accepting your gay son.

This book is informed by our personal experiences when we came out to our families and friends. Some of these questions are the ones that our moms and dads wanted to ask but simply didn't know how to; others are those that we so desperately wished they had asked.

When we came out to our families, it was an extremely emotional time. For both of our families, learning that we were gay was an uncertain, scary and difficult process. Our parents struggled to understand it. Both sets of our parents are religious and had many concerns that our sexuality went against their religious convictions. And most of all, the conversations about sexuality were incredibly difficult to initiate, and we didn't know what the right words were to use in order to say everything we wanted to say. Because of these challenges, we did a lot of research on sexuality. We decided to write this book for families who are going through the same things that we went through, and we truly believe that it can

How to Understand and Accept Your Gay Son

be helpful to you as you learn to understand and accept your son.

You have learned that your son is different from most other boys, and you might be feeling confused about what this means, worried about what this holds for his and your future, and the future of your family. You might even be fearful of potential dangers that your son faces, given the fact that he is a part of a minority group with tremendous <u>social</u>[1], <u>political</u>[2], and even <u>economic pressures</u>[3]. There might even be a part of you that finds it deeply uncomfortable that your son is attracted to other guys. Or you might fear the social stigma, ridicule or rejection of your community which you, your son and the rest of your family might be confronted with.

All of these experiences and emotions are natural, and we are here to tell you that you should not feel guilty for experiencing any of them. In fact, we, as the authors, are intimately familiar with the challenges and conflicting emotions involved as we have experienced them personally with our families as a gay couple.

In many cases, parents are not prepared to deal with their son's sexuality. Social institutions, such as schools and churches, don't often speak about diverse sexuality. While in some cases there have been some advances in sexual education, particularly in terms of helping to prevent teenage pregnancy, HIV and sexually transmitted infections (STIs), it is not yet standard procedure for schools to educate young people on issues of sexuality.

When gay individuals do come out of the closet, the family of a gay child also comes out of the closet to their friends, other family members, and possibly colleagues and other acquaintances. This book aims to provide you with information and tips that will support you as you prepare yourself to declare with confidence, "I am the proud parent of a gay son, and I couldn't be happier to love my child for who he is."

In addition, this book provides you with some very useful examples of dialogue to guide you on how to approach and initiate some challenging conversations or deal with difficult situations that might arise. These dialogues aim to provide you with the confidence, sensitivity, and understanding to engage with your son in as loving a way as possible.

For now, we are delighted that you are willing to accompany us on these important first steps as you start finding ways to respect and respond to your son's emotional needs, and as you work to strengthen the family ties so often needed during times of change. Having more information about homosexuality empowers you to shape the direction of your relationship with your son. Thank you for taking this important first step in learning to understand and accept your gay son.

What this book offers you

This book deals with all of the common questions and issues faced by a parent of a gay son, and everything is dealt with in a candid, honest and practical way. The book will offer you ideas for what to say when dealing with awkward situations such as what to say once your child has come out to you, or even if you suspect that your child is gay and want to create a supportive environment.

The book will also deal with all of the confusing, tough questions faced by parents: Is being gay a choice? Is it unnatural to be gay? How do you reconcile being gay with religious teachings? What if you are prejudiced against gay people yourself? Will your child suddenly change in ways you don't understand? Why should you ever learn to accept your child being gay?

All of these topics will be discussed, along with a host of the misconceptions and misinformation about homosexuality, in order to give you the best answers we've found in our years of research and practical, first-hand experience on this topic.

Be warned, if you are still very new to the idea of your son being gay and have not dealt with the topic of homosexuality before, there might be some parts of this book that make you very uncomfortable, and information that you might at times not enjoy reading about. However, we aim to always be educational and honest as we provide the no-nonsense answers to the questions you still have about what it means to be gay and how to deal with this new dimension in your relationship with your son.

Our main goal with this book is to make sure that your relationship with your child can remain - or begin to be - loving, supportive and close as you embark on the journey of discovery with him. You are gaining access into a part of his life that he might have been struggling with for a long time, so it's important to be sensitive and understanding throughout. But at the same time your confusion, fears, shock and even anger are all valid reactions, and the later chapters in this book will offer you some steps to working through these feelings.

How to use this book

We recommend that you read this book from cover to cover, as the book was designed so that the sections lead into one another. However, if there are only certain areas of the book that grab your interest for whatever reason, feel free to flip to that section and return to earlier sections as you choose.

Please note that the italicized terms refer to terminology that will be explained in a short glossary at the back of the book, for your convenience. Furthermore, there are scripted dialogues contained in this book, mostly in the second half, to

How to Understand and Accept Your Gay Son

offer you some guidance on how to approach your son in various scenarios. We believe that they will be a great aid in protecting your relationship with your son.

Finally, we have compiled a list of additional resources for your perusal. These include gay-positive videos, imagery, links to organisation, and other resources that we believe will be helpful, which you can also find in the final section of this book.

Chapter 1: So Where Do I Start?

What is the acronym LGBT?

LGBT stands for Lesbian, Gay, Bisexual, and Transgender.

Women who are sexually and romantically attracted to other women often self-identify as lesbians, although some of these women also identify under the more inclusive category of "gay".

Being gay means being sexually and romantically attracted to others of the same sex, and is mostly used to refer to men who are attracted to other men.

Bisexuality is a man or woman experiencing sexual and romantic attraction to both men and women.

Being transgender means being born with the body of one sex, but identifying as someone of the other sex. It refers to someone being born in the body of a man but *knowing and feeling* that they are a woman, or vice versa. It is important that you understand a very clear distinction: this has nothing to do with sexuality but is rather a gender identity. It is included in the LGBT spectrum because transgender people usually face similar discrimination and are viewed as a minority, just like lesbians, gay people and bisexuals.

As our understanding of human sexuality and gender identity expands, new acronyms have been added to the LGBT spectrum, including Q, I, A, P and others. The "Q" usually refers to those who identify as queer, a very inclusive term for those with alternative sexualities or gender identities to the majority of people. The "I" refers to intersex people (born with both male and female sexual organs, or with otherwise atypical or ambiguous sexual organs). The "A" refers to asexuals, who are people who do not have any, or have very weak, sexual attractions to either or both sexes. The "P" refers to pansexuals who are sexually and romantically attracted to people of any sex or gender identity.

As you can tell, sexual and gender identity is extremely diverse. In the 1950s, an American researcher, Alfred Kinsey, conducted a pioneering study on human sexuality. Kinsey developed a scale from 0 to 6[4] in order to explain human attraction, with 0 being exclusively heterosexual and 6 being exclusively homosexual. His research, and that of subsequent researchers, found that a significant portion[5] of the population fall somewhere between 0 and 6, and very few people fall at either extreme. Sexual identity is not always easily defined. Nowadays, there are some people who advocate for an even broader scale, and argue that there are dozens of different sexualities and gender identities. However, covering the topic in such depth is not within the scope of this book.

It is important that you do not let this new language or these variations further complicate your understanding of your son. Unless he has shared feelings about an ambiguous gender identity, it is most likely that you are dealing with a young man who identifies as a man and who is simply attracted to other men.

What is homosexuality? And what is it NOT?

It is the attraction to people of the same sex, both romantically and sexually, just as heterosexuality is attraction to people of the opposite sex, both romantically and sexually.

Being attracted to the same sex will usually be linked to an LGB identity. If your son is mostly attracted to other guys, he will usually identify as gay. This means that the person he falls in love with and perhaps eventually chooses to spend his life with will be another male.

Research suggests that biological factors, like hormones in early uterine development or genetic differences, are very important in determining sexuality, so the best answer currently is that a portion of the population is born with same sex attraction or forms it at a very early age. Some of this research will be explained in later sections with links where you can read more.

It is NOT:

There are many popular misconceptions about homosexuality, and these will be explored in the chapters of this book. To outline a few of them at the start, homosexuality is not:

- a choice
- an active rebellion against God, culture, or you as a parent
- a result of "recruitment" by other gay people
- a result of "failure" on the part of the parent
- a precursor to a lonely, promiscuous, debaucherous lifestyle
- easily recognisable and matching one stereotypical profile: although there are many tendencies and cultural aspects linked to those who identify as gay, there are no definitive characteristics which can be used to profile sexuality

Are there any signs that I can look out for to see whether my son might be gay?

Gay men are not always recognisable by certain traits or characteristics. You might imagine that gay people are generally more effeminate or have *gender nonconforming* interests, and while many gay people do show these characteristics, it is not always the case. You might be very surprised that your son is gay as he might not fit the stereotypes that you have associated with gay people at all. On the other hand you might have suspected from a young age that he is gay due to the way he talks or walks, due to his personality or because of his interests.

The simple answer is that there are no definitive signs that someone is gay. Sometimes people might even be straight but seem quite effeminate to you, so it is not useful to stereotype what being gay looks like.

It is important to note the difference between *gender identity* and *sexuality*. *Gender identity* is whether someone identifies as a man or a woman, and whether they have traits and characteristics usually associated with men and women. *Sexuality* refers to the type of sexual or romantic attractions that the person forms, as well as their thoughts and feelings concerning their sexual attraction and sex. You might identify and strongly present with traits and characteristics from one gender, such as seeing yourself as a man and having very

How to Understand and Accept Your Gay Son

traditionally masculine characteristics, and be gay. Or you might be a male who has many feminine characteristics and be straight.

Research has however found that gay men are between <u>two and four times more likely</u>[6] than straight men to show effeminate behavior or mannerisms, and about half of gay boys will have a few gender nonconforming traits, versus a tenth to a quarter of straight boys. Boys are often bullied for being "sissies" if they present these traits, and it is important for you to be very sensitive to your child's gendered behavior. This will be discussed further in later chapters.

Chapter 2: Why is my son gay?

While this is a common question, and while we feel it is important to address it, we would also like to ask you to consider the reasons why you would like this question answered. Do we ask the same questions about heterosexuality, about why your other son or daughter comes home with and dates a person of the opposite sex? Do social scientists feverishly conduct research in the hope of finding the 'causes' of heterosexuality? No, they do not. That is because heterosexuality is the perceived norm, and unlike homosexuality, people do not feel the need to question its origins or 'causes'. In other words, we do not *pathologize* heterosexuality like we often pathologize homosexuality. This can be seen as a type of heterosexual privilege enjoyed by straight people: never having to ask yourself 'why' you are the way you are, or looking for causes rooted in harmful childhood events or genetic anomalies.

So while we will offer a glimpse into the theories and evidence research has identified, we would like eventually to see you arrive at a place where you do not feel the need to investigate the 'causes' of homosexuality. But don't worry. If you're not there yet, we are here to offer you skills and tips to start making sense of some of the important issues at play.

Is it a birth defect?

The vast amount of research on sexuality so far has not been able to isolate a definitive single cause for homosexuality, and science simply does not have a conclusive answer to what makes us attracted to one group or the other. Sexuality is explained as the result of a combination of genetic, hormonal and environmental factors.[7]

It is important to remember that being gay is not a "defect", and your child might be different from the majority of people in one way, but he is still the same child that you have always known him to be. There is nothing "wrong" with him and there is no way to "cure" him. He simply has different emotional and sexual attractions and a different sexual identity to the majority of people.

Did I do something wrong as a parent?

This is a difficult question that many parents start asking themselves about their roles as parents and from personal experience we can say that it is a very important point to navigate within yourself.

The truth is that you did not do anything to "make" your child gay. Perhaps, if he told you he is gay, it means that he feels comfortable enough to reveal this important part of himself. So chances are that you are actually doing something *right* as a parent by creating a supportive environment so that your son can be honest with you about himself and his life.

There simply is no way to predict homosexuality. Gay children have come out of loving families as well as out of abusive families. They have been given positive messages about diverse sexuality in some cases, where other families have told them that all gay people are disgusting and will go to hell. There is, as far as the research tells us, no way to know which people will be gay[8] besides a few biological factors discussed below. There is no amount of shaming, intolerance or negative messages that you can give to your child that will cause him to no longer be gay, and disowning him because of it will only rob you of a relationship with your own child and will not change his sexuality.

Is it because his father was absent? Is it because he is too close to his mother?

None of these factors have any bearing on sexuality. There is no statistically significant link[9] between absent fathers and homosexuality. There are many gay men who are close with their mothers, and culturally a large amount of gay men show a greater fondness for *heterosocial* relationships versus straight men, which are friendships and platonic bonding with people of the opposite sex. However, there are also many cases of distant, absent or rejecting mothers who have gay sons.

These ideas come from outdated theories that saw homosexuality as a mental disorder caused by certain types of parental involvement, such as the theories of Freud and others. Rigorous studies[10] and biological evidence have shown this not to be the case.

A variety of factors are involved, but it is no one's "fault". There is absolutely no real evidence that a certain host of environmental factors will result in someone being gay, and this is no reason to be more distant or less loving of your son in order to try and change his identity.

Is there anything I can do now to change him?

No. While there are cases of "ex-gay" people (discussed below), and in some cases sexuality can be very fluid, you can be pretty sure that once your child has identified as gay he has probably gone on a long journey with many challenges and realized that he can't deny his feelings anymore. Sexuality is something that becomes a fundamental part of our identity. Think about your own sexuality: do you think it would be possible to simply *change* the fact that you are attracted to the opposite sex? All of the evidence suggests[11] that the most people can really do is to deny their sexuality but they cannot change it, and this denial usually comes with a great amount of self-hatred, depression and in many cases suicide[12]. The only way to live a healthy, honest, happy life for your child will be once he finds an accepting community (which you can be a part of) and once he learns to accept himself.

What about those "ex-gay" people I have been hearing about?

There is a lot of evidence that ex-gay ministries and programs are merely trying to recondition behavior and to force people to deny that they are really gay. In fact, a large number of people who claim to have been "cured" of homosexuality eventually admit that they were merely lying[13], forcing themselves to believe that they could suppress their true feelings and desires. It is extremely, *extremely* unlikely that your son will be any different, and you can be very close to

How to Understand and Accept Your Gay Son

certain that putting him through this kind of program will only cause him more shame about his identity and be ineffective in really changing him. Please read this section carefully if you are considering any type of "conversion" or "reparative" therapy.

These programs are very harmful. They have ranged from torturous activities like shock therapy, "exorcisms" and inducing vomiting, to extremely hateful messages spread in religious interventions. None of these have been shown to have any real effect on "converting" homosexuals. The American Psychological Association, the American Medical Association and many other mental health bodies condemn these types of "treatments"[14].

Once someone becomes "ex-gay", their life can be incredibly difficult and painful, not only for the gay person, but also for their partners in opposite-sex relationships. Their partners will never really share the level of love and intimacy that could be gained from a relationship based on mutual attraction where both partners can really love one another. Would you ever want to be married to someone who was forcing himself or herself to be attracted to you? There are numerous stories[15] which you can find on the internet about people who were forced to be ex-gay or who felt so rejected in their lives that they chose to deny who they really are. These programs have even been banned[16] in many parts of the developed world due to how much distress they cause to gay people who participate in them. We can't stress this point enough: please **do not** consider these programs at all, as they are likely to lead to much pain and further self-hatred for your child. A small amount of research on your part will show you how damaging they can be, and how many lives they have destroyed, both for the person who is attracted to the same sex as well as any opposite-sex partners they have. If there were a real way to alter homosexuality, it would have been scientifically documented and widely publicized by now, and it would not be based on pseudoscience and lies, or cause as much damage as ex-gay ministries. Simply put: based on the evidence, these programs do not work and are potentially very harmful.

Is it a choice to be gay?

This is a very common idea about being gay. People claim that it is a lifestyle choice[17] caused either by wanting to be different or by simple confusion. Many people assume that gay people can choose to be straight if they want to, or that they could simply go through their lives without acting on their romantic or sexual feelings even if they are gay. Many people who regard it as a "sin" to be gay compare it to other acts like murder, theft or even child molestation, and say that they can choose not to act on it just like others choose not to murder, steal or abuse children.

When we examine these assumptions, they are clearly not true and are very damaging.

Very few gay people regard it as a choice, and the reasons should be obvious: why would someone choose to be discriminated against socially and legally, and suffer social stigma like childhood bullying, the potential rejection of family and friends, isolation from their religious communities, and even the higher prevalence of suicide and HIV infection, if they could choose the alternative and be straight? In fact, almost every gay person you will meet will tell you that they would have chosen to be straight or that they *tried* to choose being straight at some point in their lives. But sexuality doesn't work that way. It is not a choice.

Even some people who are in favour of homosexuality will use the refrain: "it's their choice, they can live however they want." Even in an otherwise accepting community, this phrasing is dangerous since it makes it seem like the gay person could choose to be something other than who they really are. Being gay is his identity, not his choice.

The assumption rests on the fact that people consider being straight to be "normal" and being gay to be "abnormal", and thus "choosing" to be gay is trying to deny convention and what is normal. But if you start to understand your gay child as being inherently and innately gay, and realize that being gay is a part of his identity, you will understand that it is not his choice to have the identity that he has. It is no more a choice for your son to be gay than it is for you to be straight.

We don't control every aspect of ourselves, and we can't choose alternatives to parts of our identity or preferences. For example: did you choose your favourite colour? Can you change which colour you like best simply by deciding it? Did you "choose" whether to enjoy certain foods and to dislike others? Did you "choose" how to feel about your parents or your children? Did you "choose" to be attracted to your partner, someone you pass in the street or a good-looking film star even though you were not attracted to them initially? Or is it simply something that happens for lots of complex reasons?

Sexual attraction and romantic feelings are tied to our biology and psychology, and sexual identity is not a logical, rational aspect of our being based on choice. Whether the attraction is heterosexual or homosexual, if someone sexually excites us, or if we feel strong romantic feelings towards someone, this is not something we decide. It just happens. We have involuntary responses when we are around someone we find attractive, and we can't instruct ourselves to have those responses if we do not naturally find someone attractive.

The idea of "choice" also assumes that it is easy, or even possible, to redirect your affections to others who you do not find attractive at all. If you are or have ever been in love, imagine a world where someone told you that you are no longer allowed to love that person, and where you have to only love someone from a group of people you are not sexually or romantically attracted to, like someone from the same sex. Would you be able to "choose" to change who you love?

What are the biological reasons for my son being gay?

The best research shows that there are many different influences. Strong evidence suggests that genes play a role[18], and some genes have already been isolated which might be linked to homosexuality. In studies of twins and brothers, there are strong indications that homosexuality is genetic[19] and that a higher number of twins[20] will have the same sexual orientation versus brothers who gestate separately. But this does not seem to be the whole answer.

Recent studies have also linked homosexuality to high female fertility[21] in the same family, the birth order[22] of the child and how this affects hormones released in the uterus (the more older brothers a child has, the more likely he is to be gay), differences in brain structure[23] and responses to pheromones[24]. There is a wealth of research which supports the idea that biological factors are important in determining sexuality, and thus it is safe to draw the conclusion that people who are gay are born gay or have their sexuality formed very early in life, and do not become gay through external influences later in life. However, for some people, it might take them a long time to accept these same-sex attractions.

What do the experts say about being gay?

For a long time, homosexuality was considered a mental disorder. In fact, homosexuality as a mental illness was removed from the *Diagnostic and Statistical Manual* (DSM) by the American Psychiatric Association (APA) as long ago as 1973. The DSM is the main resource for psychologists and psychiatrists when it comes to diagnosing mental disorders. The APA was soon followed in declassifying homosexuality as a mental disorder by the American Medical Association, the American Psychological Association, the American Psychoanalytic Association, the American Academy of Pediatrics and the National Association of Social Workers, among others. Those are a lot of mental health and medical professional bodies that denounce the classification of homosexuality as being an illness, disorder or dysfunction.

What does this tell us? It shows that the highly trained academics, professionals and practitioners of mental and physical health are telling us that *there is nothing wrong with you if you are gay*. Even if you should decide to take your child to a therapist's office, if the therapist is ethical, responsible, and operating within the codes of conduct of the professional bodies to which they belong, they should assure you that there is nothing wrong with your son and that you didn't do anything wrong to make him gay.

Your son has nothing psychologically wrong with him to 'explain' his homosexuality. Does this mean that you can sit back and relax about your son's mental health? Unfortunately, if your son is gay, there is a good chance that he is struggling with his mental health, not because of his sexuality but because of the homophobic pressures and bullying that he may be exposed to.

How your son's mental health is affected

Statistically, gay men confront greater challenges to mental health relative to the general population. Common struggles include depression, anxiety, low self-esteem, and suicide ideation. Alarmingly, gay men are four times[25] as likely as their heterosexual counterparts to commit suicide. A reasonable question to be asking is: why? Why are gay men so much more likely to harm themselves? What is creating this depression, this anxiety, and this desire to self-harm?

Some people lay the blame at the feet of the young gay men themselves. They claim that to be homosexual is to be mentally ill by definition, and that is why gay men are more prone to self-harming behaviors. This, of course, is blatantly false.

As mentioned above, mental health professionals do not consider homosexuality to be a mental illness.

What does negatively impact the mental health of homosexual men, is the often merciless bullying[26] many of them experience from a very young age. Young boys who demonstrate gender nonconforming behavior are often identified as being gay, regardless of how they *self-identify*. Oftentimes this type of bullying occurs for prolonged periods of time. Bullying causes fear, erodes self-esteem, causes constant anxiety, and disrupts one's social life and academic performance. But most importantly, when left unaddressed, gay people might fall into a state of *learned helplessness*, where they do not perceive themselves to have enough influence over their dilemma to effect any change. Such a state of learned helplessness often leads to depression. When your life is marked by frequent violent encounters, be it physical or verbal, you live in a constant state of fear and anxiety. When you do not perceive yourself to be able to escape your disabling environment, you might fall into a state of depression.

When all attempts at escaping the bullying seemed to have failed, then such a state of hopelessness easily devolves into depression. Depression is often a precursor for *suicidal ideation* or actual suicide attempts.

Now before we get ahead of ourselves, remember that many gay teens do not respond to their environment in this way and that regular, honest conversations with your son is the best way to gauge his emotional state.

In our experience in counselling young gay men, it is usually the lack of acceptance and the rejection of parents that they find the most traumatic in their journey to self-acceptance. It is the sense of being misunderstood, being rejected, being told they are unacceptable and ultimately unlovable, that is so hard to bear for young gay men. It is okay for you as a parent to feel scared, lonely, and confused, but you should consider it your parental duty to explore honestly and without reservation all of these conflicting emotions. We recommend investigating resources located within your community. There might be a PFLAG (Parents, Family and Friends of Lesbians and Gays) chapter in your community, or a similar support or educational group. You might want to confide in family and friends. You might seek out the help of a counselor. There are also countless discussion boards and resources online; you can find some of these in the resources section at the end of this book. Most importantly, adopt a proactive approach to understanding and ultimately accepting this aspect of your son's identity. Research shows[27] that a strong supportive network in the coming out process of young gay men acts as a protective factor against mental health problems during this time when your son is at his most vulnerable. If he senses your unconditional support, you will help safeguard him against depression and anxiety.

Importantly, do not place too much pressure on yourself to be 100% accepting and all-embracing of your son's sexuality overnight. That might be unrealistic when you have your own confusion and perhaps even spiritual uncertainties to deal with. Rather, try to make the commitment that you will do your best to understand your son and that you will access information that is objective and in the best interest of you and your son's relationship. As valuable as the Internet can be, there are also voices that want to be heard that are not in the best interest of your child or the relationship between the two of you.

By being informed, challenging your own preconceptions about gay men, and offering unconditional love and support to your son, you will be fulfilling your duty in safeguarding him against any needless suffering. Honest and affirming dialogue will provide you and your son with the platform to engage meaningfully with each other as you navigate the newness of his sexual identity.

Chapter 3: Homophobia: The deadly threat to your son's mental health

What is homophobia?

Homophobia can be defined as the fear and loathing of homosexual people. Those who are homophobic will usually express these feelings through certain behaviors: ridiculing gay people, shaming or judging them, avoiding them, discriminating against them, and even through violence. In some places, homophobia is so prevalent and powerful that laws[28] are put in place to criminalize gay relationships or gender nonconforming behavior. In fact, in almost a dozen countries worldwide gay people can be legally sentenced to death[29] simply for being gay. Many gay young people report being bullied at school, and there is even "corrective rape"[30] of gay people, which is ignorantly believed to cure them of homosexuality through sexual assault. This, of course, is a damaging myth, since there is no way to "cure" one's sexual identity.

What gives rise to such intense feelings of dislike and fear? There are several theories that are offered to explain homophobia. The theories range from often untested assumptions of what gay men do in the bedroom, to the fear of femininity in men, to the fear of some straight men that gay men will hit on them, to the fear of HIV. Many people also rely on religious doctrine in order to support their homophobia, and as the basis for their understanding of gay people (see chapter 4). It will be useful to examine each of these factors in a bit more detail.

1. Homophobia as expressed by the fear of gay sex

One of the examples of straight privilege is the advantage enjoyed by heterosexual people of not having a private, sensitive aspect of their identity be constantly *sexualized* or scandalized. Think about it. When you meet a person, it is unlikely that you are considering what they do to whom in the privacy of their own bedroom, precisely because you have not identified him by his sexuality. Should you learn that he has a girlfriend or wife, or a female partner, chances are still slim that you are considering what sexual behaviors he might be practising. However, if you meet a person, and it emerges through casual discussion that he is gay, for some reason many of us find ourselves veering into thinking of his sexual behavior. Absurdly, it is not uncommon for gay men to be

How to Understand and Accept Your Gay Son

asked by relative strangers what their favourite sexual position is.

Of course, one of the most taboo and widely scandalized sexual acts is anal sex. Many people are extremely uncomfortable with even talking about it, yet it is still used as a reason for a lot of hatred against gay people. We will discuss the topic here in order to give you some information to counter homophobia. However, if the conversation makes you very uncomfortable and if you have no interest in thinking about it, you might want to skip to the next section below.

People often consider anal sex to be practised exclusively by gay men. While anal sex is a common sexual behavior amongst gay men, it would be incorrect to believe that only gay men participate in this sexual behavior, or that all gay men[31] practise it. Up to 1 out of every 4[32] heterosexual couples have practised anal sex, or practise it regularly, and among young people, 44% of straight men and 36% of straight women have tried anal sex before, according to the Center for Disease Control (CDC[33]). If so many straight people are engaging in anal sex, why is it used as a weapon against gay people? The answer is that people really have a problem with men being intimate with other men.

In many societies, sex is a topic that is shrouded in shame, secrecy, guilt, and repression. Taking a topic which is already difficult for many people to discuss openly, and narrow it down to a taboo act like anal sex, and most people would prefer to look the other way. Anal sex is seen as "unnatural" as it does not lead to reproduction, but for that matter isn't oral sex, the use of sex toys, heavy petting or other forms of sex which do not involve vaginal penetration by a penis the same?

As with many topics that are left to the imagination, rather than openly discussed, many of the [assumptions made about anal sex are false](...)[34]. It is beyond the scope of this book to counter each misconception, but it should be clear that just like other forms of sex, anal sex can be a harmless, intimate, personal act to be enjoyed between consenting partners, regardless of gender or sexuality. Also, just as there are heterosexual people who enjoy anal sex, there are also homosexual men who do not enjoy or participate in it. The key here is to appreciate the inherent diversity within every group of people, and to realize that what happens in someone else's bed is not the business of anyone else.

While gay sex might be a topic that causes many people discomfort, the sexual practices between a couple are private and should not be the basis for hatred towards people.

2. Homophobia as expressed by the fear of femininity in men

Research shows that it is not the gender conforming gay boy who gets teased most at school. Rather, it is the gender nonconforming boy[35], whether or not he self-identifies as gay, who suffers the most at the hands of bullies. So the boy who might be slight in build, has a high-pitched voice, has more feminine body language, and a somewhat feminine step in his walk - that boy is likely to attract the attention of bullies. It isn't the boy that plays rough contact sports, who has a deep voice, and who has a strong physical build that gets bullied. Why is this the case?

We live in a society that prizes the perception of masculinity over femininity. This can be seen across many domains. Take for instance the workplace. A man and woman are employed at the same organisation, in the same title and position, perform the exact same tasks and duties, and perform to the same level of satisfaction of their boss. Is the man or the woman more likely to be paid more? According to research, the woman only earns 78c to every $1 the man earns[36] for the same work and skill level.

Even at a young age we can see this gender difference take place. While it's considered cute and positive for a girl to be a "tomboy", it is an insult for a boy to be a "sissy"[37].

You may ask what that has to do with your gay son. Certain stereotypes exist about gay men which have served to entrench their stigmatized status in society. However, perhaps it is not the stereotypes that are the problem, but it is rather society's perception of what these stereotypes represent that is the problem.

Can any one person be considered to be completely feminine or completely masculine in her or his *gender identity*? If you are a woman and you live in a society that dictates fixing a car to be purely a masculine activity, yet one weekend you do a good job of repairing your own car after some tinkering and researching, ask yourself the question: am I really that different than that boy who has a slight feminine gait? Think of a friend, colleague, family member, or other acquaintance that speaks in a somewhat deeper, more masculine voice than what traditionally befits her gender: how different is she from our hypothetical boy with the slight feminine gait? In a similar vein, if you are a man and you are left at home to take care of your children if your female partner has to leave town, and are tasked with traditionally female household tasks such as doing the laundry, cooking, and cleaning, does this make you less of a man?

Traces of femininity in boys are stringently policed by society[38]: parents are more likely to 'discipline' their sons for playing with dolls or wishing to dress up in 'girl's' clothing, than their 'tomboy' daughter who enjoys climbing trees and befriends more boys than girls. We suggest that this has to do with society considering so-called masculine pursuits to be more honorable and more deserving of praise than feminine pursuits. While we cannot change entrenched views on gender roles in society, we can raise our children to pursue whatever natural interests they have: be it playing with dolls as a boy, or playing football as a girl.

It is our belief that only when we raise our children to embrace their interests and to pursue them, without shaming them or inflicting guilt upon them, that we will be making decisive moves to help eradicate homophobia. After all, by valuing your son's complete spectrum of interests and activities he wishes to participate in, you are doing your bit to challenge gender norms. And challenging gender norms means challenging systems that are in place which hurt your gay son.

3. Homophobia due to fear that gay men will hit on straight men

There is a common misconception that gay men are uncontrollably sexual all the time, and are sexual predators who will chase after any men they encounter. This is obviously nonsense. Research shows[39] that gay men are not any more promiscuous than straight men, and most gay men are not interested in pursuing straight men at all.

Recent research from a popular dating site has found that only a tiny fraction of gay men seek out straight partners (0,6%), and most only search for other gay or bisexual partners. Gay men also showed very similar amounts of sexual partners to straight men on the site.

Gay men are no different from straight men in terms of interest in sex or the amounts of sexual partners.

In repressed conditions where homosexuality is criminalized or carries strong social stigma, there usually are higher instances of unsafe, destructive or hypersexualized patterns. In the US, since gay marriage became legal in most states, the number of sexual partners for gay men per year has actually gone *down*[40].

This evidence suggests that creating an inclusive society might begin to equalize sexual patterns more, and might help to reduce risky sexual behavior. This is true especially for men who feel trapped into pretending to be straight, partnering with women, and then still engaging in sex with men, which is a phenomenon known as being on the "down-low". This is a very common cause of the spread of HIV in homophobic communities, and is common with many "ex-gay" people. Not only this, it is further evidence of the dangers associated with gay men who are not provided the support and nurturing environment to embrace their attractions honestly.

Gay men are not animals, and they are not mindlessly attracted to all other men. Picture yourself walking into a bar: do you find every person there attractive? Do you want to be intimate with everyone you see? Neither will your son.

Mostly gay men are just as insecure as straight men and won't be as bold as to approach someone who will probably reject them; consequently, straight men are usually off limits. Of course, just like with some straight men, there are loutish, disrespectful gay men who will catcall and aggressively pursue someone who is not interested, even if they are straight. These men are generally a very small minority. This behavior is not because they are gay, it is because they are rude.

4. Homophobia due to the fear of HIV

HIV was originally known as GRID, or Gay-Related Immune Deficiency, when little was known about the disease. Since many gay men presented with HIV in the US due to poor knowledge of the risks of unsafe sex, especially receptive anal sex which carries the highest risk of HIV infection (up to 18 times[41] the infection rate of vaginal sex), and HIV tests were not widely accessible, gay men often spread HIV without knowing it.

In countries like the US, HIV is still concentrated in men who have sex with men - a public health term used to place emphasis on sexual behavior as opposed to sexual identity, since MSM might identify as either gay, bisexual, straight or none of the above. About half of the people living with HIV[42] in the US and the majority of new infections each year are MSM. While it is important to address these alarming statistics, we need to encourage you to understand the reasons behind them rather than stigmatize gay people as being dangerous carriers of HIV.

An estimated 20% of gay men[43] in US cities are HIV positive, so there is a much higher prevalence than the general population, and thus the risks of MSM being infected are far higher. The prevalence is also due to anal sex being riskier than other forms of sex, leading to a higher rate of HIV infection. It is also caused by secretive, risky "down-low" sex, or other forms of risky sex due to repressive, homophobic norms. So a gay man who has the same number of sexual partners as a straight man or a woman, but does not use protection, will be *much more likely* to be infected with HIV due to these risk factors.

The prevalence of HIV among gay men does not mean that HIV is caused by gay people or is a curse on gay people. It simply is a result of the higher amount of risk factors involved for MSM. It is thus not a curse on any group of people, but a virus which mutated to survive and spread in humans. There are biological, not spiritual or metaphysical, reasons for the existence of HIV, and the rest of the things you may be hearing are simply myths and dangerously ignorant rumours.

Some forms of sex are riskier, and a large number of potential partners are already infected for MSM. Therefore they need to be a lot more careful than other groups, should be tested more often, and should always use condoms with new or non-exclusive sexual partners. The risks are real, but the stigma and myths are based on falsehoods.

However, in the rest of the world, the vast majority of those with HIV live in Sub-Saharan Africa[44], and mostly poor, straight, black women are infected. This is due to these women not having agency in sexual matters and reproductive health, and therefore not being able to choose when to have sex with their male partners or insist on the use of condoms. Other factors like poor education, sexual violence, straight men having many sexual partners and thus spreading HIV to many women, social stigma linked to getting tested, and the inability to access healthcare facilities also lead to the spread of HIV among poor women. It is no longer a "gay disease", although MSM still are an at-risk population in all parts of the world due to the factors discussed above.

Let's just state this clearly: the vast majority of gay men do not have AIDS and will not contract the virus in their lifetimes. Your son will need to be aware of the risks involved but with the necessary information he can protect himself and maintain a healthy sexual life.

You can find more information about HIV in the second section of this book ("Accepting Your Gay Son"), where we provide some facts about the virus and how it spreads and ideas of what to say to discuss HIV with your son.

Internalized homophobia

Part of our work in the education and public health fields is to conduct sensitization training to make people more aware of the struggles of gay people. We often conduct an activity which has been dubbed 'Those People'. Before we explain the relevance and importance of this activity, we would like you to complete it yourself. It is designed so that one can better empathize with gay men around the topics of homophobia, stigma, and the feeling of otherness.

How to Understand and Accept Your Gay Son

Instructions:

1. Sit quietly. Close your eyes and think of an aspect of your identity that is different, and makes you feel like an outsider, stigmatized or oppressed.

2. If possible, listen as the following scenario, "Those People", is read by somebody that you trust. Otherwise, read it yourself, and pay close attention to the words, making an effort to put yourself in the shoes of "those people".

3. <u>During the reading imagine that the passage is about you. In place of the words "those people", think of an aspect of your identity that has made you feel stigmatised, oppressed or like an outsider.</u>

<u>Those People</u>

Imagine, if you will, growing up hearing about a group of people that exist in society who are "**defective**" and that are all "**going to hell**" because of who they are and who they love.

You rarely see "**those people**" represented on television, magazines, or in movies, and when you do they are usually the humorous characters that are viewed as unusual or silly. They are not characters, they are caricatures.

There may be a rumour that one actually lives in your neighbourhood or that someone has one in her/his family, but your parents forbid you to even talk about that possibility.

Imagine the children at school telling jokes about the way **"those people"** talk and act and you even hear jokes about diseases that some of **"those people"** get from doing **"inappropriate"** or **"immoral"** things.

You see news reports and "made for TV movies" about some of **"those people"** being beaten, tortured, and killed for no other reason than being who they are.

In class you learn about laws that restrict **"those people"** from having the same basic human and civil rights and legal protections as everyone else in society.

You also hear rumours that **"those people"** should not be left alone with children because many of them are sexual predators who will sexually exploit the young.

Now imagine thinking and feeling that you yourself might be one of **"those people"**...What would you do? How would you survive?

How did you find this activity? Imagine all of these messages above that are being transmitted by the media and social institutions, such as the church and school, about a core part of your identity. Through no fault of your own, and not by choice (see Chapter 2), you are considered defective, deserving of going to hell, portrayed as ridiculous caricatures on television, suspected of being a pedophile although there is no evidence to suggest this, you learn that people in your position are tortured and killed throughout the world simply because of who they are, and you are denied basic civil and human rights.

More often than not, your son will start to absorb these messages, and begin to internalise the stigma and homophobia. As discussed in Chapter 2, this can be very damaging for his self-esteem, lead to anxiety and depression, and suicidal ideation if not suicide attempts. When your son starts to hate himself for being gay or fear that part of his identity, and hate other gay people as well, this is known as *internalized homophobia*. Your son may actually be carrying negative messages about his identity inside of himself, only compounding the messages he hears from others in his surroundings.

How can I protect my child from homophobia?

Now that you understand how incredibly harmful and widespread homophobia can be, and that it is based on so many myths and misconceptions, your instinct might be to ask: how can I safeguard my son from this? What can I do to stop homophobia?

Sadly, your child will very likely face some form of homophobia in his life. He might be bullied at school, or face people who ridicule him, discriminate against him or even threaten him with violence.

The best thing that you can do for your son is to instil a strong sense in him that he is a good, multidimensional and worthwhile person, and provide him with tools to deal with issues he might face. You can also make sure that he has a safe and loving environment at home where he can be himself, as this will go a long way to boosting his self-esteem. Additionally, if you fear that his mental health has been affected, you should consider counselling for him and perhaps even for your family.

Finally, when you have learned to accept and embrace your son's identity, you might want to become an advocate for gay rights and gay dignity, as well as publicly and proudly voicing the fact that you oppose homophobia, and standing up against it whenever you notice it in your surroundings.

Chapter 4: What does God say?

Why does the Bible seem to condemn homosexuality?

This is an important question, as so much discomfort and unfamiliarity with homosexuality is often linked to people's interpretation of what religions say. As we, the authors, have been raised in Christian households, we are intimately aware of the harmful impact that certain interpretations of homosexuality in scripture can have on a young man's self-esteem, mental health, and sense of self-worth. In this chapter we'll examine what the Bible says about homosexuality, looking at each instance for what it really is and not for how these verses are often misused in order to deter the acceptance of gay men.

For those who do hold the position that homosexuality goes against God's teachings, it is not within our power to change those perspectives outright. If you choose not to engage with this topic and to skip this section, we completely understand this decision. You need to decide what is best for your own spiritual beliefs, and perhaps discussing these verses might be offensive to you. But if you would like more clarity about exactly what the Bible says about being gay, and how gay people have found ways to reconcile their sexuality and their religious beliefs, this section might be very helpful to you. You will begin to see that Christianity really *does not condemn* homosexuality if it is based on Biblical teachings.

We would like to provide you with more inclusive, understanding, and loving interpretations of the Bible which many Biblical scholars hold. We believe that a loving God would want a loving interpretation of His words which does not exclude anyone from His message simply based on one aspect of their identity. We would also like to clearly demonstrate to you that you and your son can continue to have a strong relationship with God despite your son's homosexuality. In fact, it is even possible that with time you will view your son's homosexuality as a God-given part of his identity that you would not want to change if given the choice. That might sound far-fetched to you right now, but many people who have started this journey towards greater understanding and acceptance of their son's sexual identity have come to see it as an invaluable and precious part of what makes him who he is, and therefore what it is that you love about him.

It is beyond the scope of this book to do justice to religions other than those based on the Bible, as this is beyond our frame of experience. We ask you, if you are from another faith, to please do some research of your own in order to reconcile these tensions, but to read through this chapter nonetheless as we deal with how religions and cultures generally approach homosexuality.

The information in this chapter is taken from a multitude of reputable sources and from the teachings of religious leaders and Biblical scholars, which you can consult yourself for a more detailed discussion. We are not experts on religion, but have read widely in the field, and we present the work of experts here. While we are not trying to change your religious beliefs, we are hoping to offer you avenues in which to reconcile your faith with the reality of having a gay son. We really do not want to offend or challenge your beliefs, but rather just to offer you another option on how to interpret the Word of God so that you can build a strong relationship with your son. Our sources are listed below, and the messages from them will be given throughout this chapter:

For the Bible Tells Me So (documentary)[45]

God and the Gay Christian (book)[46]

What the Bible Really Says about Homosexuality (book)[47]

The Bible's Yes to Same-Sex Marriage: An Evangelical's Change of Heart (book)[48]

God and the Gay Christian (video)[49]

The Bible and Homosexuality (Wikipedia)[50]

Gay Christian 101 (website)[51]

Grant Andrews & Malan van der Walt

Religious Tolerance (website)[52]

Did all cultures and all religions always hate LGBT people?

Before we begin, it would be useful to consider the term 'homosexuality' and its origins, because how we see sexual diversity today is not how the authors of the Bible understood it at the time of its writing. While most of us are familiar with the term homosexuality, not many of us are aware of the fact that it is, historically speaking, a term which has only recently become commonly used.

The term 'homosexuality' was only coined in the late 19th century[53], and only in subsequent years has this idea been widely used. So while same-sex sexual behavior has been occurring across all cultures around the world, it is only relatively recent that people have understood the idea that being primarily attracted to the same sex can be a legitimate reality for a large number of people (between 1 and 10 percent of all people, according to different estimates, and an average of about 3.8% of the US population[54]).

In fact, many cultures have documented socially accepted cases of homosexual relationships[55]: in pre-colonial Africa there were many cases of men taking male lovers, South America had instances of homosexuality and transgenderism before colonial conquest, ancient Persia was permissive towards same-sex relationships, and many native Americans had the concept of being "two-spirited" people, those who were seen as having male and female spirits, and these individuals would often marry someone of the same sex. In Europe, civilizations like Ancient Rome and Greece also had many documented occurrences of socially accepted same-sex relations. These few examples show that there is nothing "unusual" about homosexuality. It was not fundamentally hated by all people, and it occurred all around the world. In fact, some reports show that up to three quarters of cultures[56] throughout history showed permissive attitudes towards some forms of homosexuality or transgenderism. Negative attitudes towards sexual diversity are not "natural", but they are learned based on our culture, time and society, and these attitudes are changeable.

Now that we know that we have only been grappling with the idea of sexual orientation for a short time, let's examine the fact that the Bible was written thousands of years ago without the understanding that homosexuality is a legitimate, widespread sexuality.

What does the Bible really say?

1. Leviticus 18 and 20 say:

"You shall not lie with a male as with a woman; it is an abomination."

"If a man lies with a male as with a woman, both of them have committed an abomination; they shall surely be put to death; their blood is upon them."

2. In Genesis, the story of the destruction of Sodom and Gomorrah has been linked to the desire of the townsmen to rape the angels God has sent to visit Lot. This has been interpreted as evidence that God condemns homosexuality. A very similar story is found in Judges 19.

3. In 1 Corinthians 6: 9-11, Paul the Apostle wrote:

"Know ye not that the unrighteous shall not inherit the kingdom of God? Be not deceived: neither fornicators, nor idolaters, nor adulterers, nor effeminate, nor abusers of themselves with mankind, Nor thieves, nor covetous, nor drunkards, nor revilers, nor extortioners, shall inherit the kingdom of God. And such were some of you: but ye are washed, but ye are sanctified, but ye are justified in the name of the Lord Jesus, and by the Spirit of our God."

How to Understand and Accept Your Gay Son

The two categories translated as "effeminate" and "abusers of themselves with mankind" are often understood as gay men.

4. In 1 Timothy 1: 8-11, Paul explains:

"But we know that the law is good, if a man use it lawfully; Knowing this, that the law is not made for a righteous man, but for the lawless and disobedient, for the ungodly and for sinners, for unholy and profane, for murderers of fathers and murderers of mothers, for manslayers, For whoremongers, for them that defile themselves with mankind, for menstealers, for liars, for perjured persons, and if there be any other thing that is contrary to sound doctrine; According to the glorious gospel of the blessed God, which was committed to my trust."

The line "them that defile themselves with mankind" is viewed as a condemnation of homosexuals.

5. In Romans 1: 26-27, Paul again says:

"For this cause God gave them up unto vile affections: for even their women did change the natural use into that which is against nature: And likewise also the men, leaving the natural use of the woman, burned in their lust one toward another; men with men working that which is unseemly, and receiving in themselves that recompense of their error which was meet."

It seems pretty clear that the God hates gay people, right?

The most important thing to remember in this discussion is that the Bible, as well as interpretations and translations of it, are all set within particular cultural contexts. The way people read the Bible today is very different from the way it was read throughout history. There are also many translations of the Bible which vastly alter the interpretation of passages. Especially the passages above, which are sometimes translated much more harshly to condemn homosexuality, and sometimes in much more nuanced ways which take stock of the fact that cultural context has a lot to do with what was written. Even if one sees the Bible as the direct words of God, remember that someone still had to write those words down in a language that was filled with linguistic limitations, and then someone else translated them into the language you understand, and each of those links in the chain could cause problems with meaning.

These are the only six instances (if Judges and Genesis are counted as two) that can even be vaguely linked to homosexuality in the Bible (although people do try and link so many other passages to homosexuality). But to counter these verses, there are also a multitude of passages in the Bible which seem to be affirming and even embracing of homoerotic desires and relationships. Even Jesus has something to say about this. And remember, he never said anything to *condemn* homosexuality.

For example, David and Jonathan, in 1 Samuel 18:1, could even be seen as engaging in a type of gay union:

"And it came to pass, when he had made an end of speaking unto Saul, that the soul of Jonathan was knit with the soul of David, and Jonathan loved him as his own soul."

David later says to Jonathan in 2 Samuel 1:26:

"I am distressed for thee, my brother Jonathan: very pleasant hast thou been unto me: thy love to me was wonderful, passing the love of women."

Another relationship interpreted as demonstrating homosexual attraction was between Ruth and Naomi in Ruth 1: 16-17 where Ruth says to Naomi:

"Where you go I will go, and where you stay I will stay. Your people will be my people and your God my God. Where you die I will die, and there I will be buried. May the Lord deal with me, be it ever so severely, if even death separates you and me. "

These words are often used in wedding ceremonies today.

Jesus himself, in a discussion of divorce in Matthew 19: 9-12, explains:

> "And I say to you, whoever divorces his wife, except for immorality, and marries another woman commits adultery." The disciples said to Him, "If the relationship of the man with his wife is like this, it is better not to marry." But He said to them, "Not all men can accept this statement, but only those to whom it has been given." For there are eunuchs who were born that way from their mother's womb; and there are eunuchs who were made eunuchs by men; and there are also eunuchs who made themselves eunuchs for the sake of the kingdom of heaven. He who is able to accept this, let him accept it."

This passage is widely understood to refer to homosexuality, and Jesus seems to be explaining that some men are born without the inclination to marry a woman. The term translated as "eunuch", according to many Biblical scholars, has a very broad range of meanings, and might simply refer to those who do not have opposite-sex attractions. So Jesus himself might have been very understanding and accepting of gay people.

These instances should show you that the Bible is not as fundamentally opposed to homosexuality as we have all been led to believe. As we discuss the previous six passages which seem to condemn homosexuality, you should keep this in mind.

What are the other interpretations of the way the Bible "condemns" homosexuality?

Now let's discuss each of the passages above individually looking at how Biblical scholars have understood them.

1. **Leviticus 18 and 20 say:**

"You shall not lie with a male as with a woman; it is an abomination."

"If a man lies with a male as with a woman, both of them have committed an abomination; they shall surely be put to death; their blood is upon them."

The Leviticus passages were written with the migration of the Israelites into Canaan, and represent their culture shock at the pagan rituals in the new land where temple prostitution and even incest were practised. Most of the rules in Leviticus were only applicable to the Levites, or Jewish priests and anointed religious leaders from the clan of Levi, in order for them to remain pure. Most of them can be understood as trying both to protect a group of people and to make sure that they reproduced optimally in a hostile foreign land. In fact, many different things which are now perfectly acceptable were also "abominations" in Leviticus, punishable by death or damnation. Examples include the eating of fat, failing to include salt in offerings to God, touching an unclean animal, letting your hair become unkempt (punished by death), eating shellfish, going to church within a month after giving birth, having sex with a woman during her period, and many, many more. These passages do not even give penalties for more serious offences such as stealing, lying, or selling someone as a slave.

It is important to note that most Christians do not apply the many rules set forth in Leviticus to their everyday lives, and not many of these rules have formed part of church doctrines. These rules were understood as specific cultural practices for a specific context, not as unbreakable laws from God. There were at least 76 rules laid out in Leviticus, and people only seem to focus or care about the one which seems to condemn homosexuality instead of the many other "abominations" like trimming your beard or not brushing your hair. We suggest that this is due to homophobia, and not due to people really fearing the wrath of God for this "abomination" when they freely practise and accept the other "abominations" set forth in Leviticus.

2. **The story of Sodom and Gomorrah, found in Genesis:**

Most Biblical scholars agree that angels are sexless. Although the masculine linguistic construction is used to refer to all biblical angels and they are often given male names or clothing, this is understood as demonstrating their authority in patriarchal societies, but they are seen as neither male nor female.

Thus, the threat of rape of the two angels in the story of Lot is not the threat of men having sex with men, but rather of people *sexually assaulting creatures that are pure*.

The crime of Sodom and Gomorrah was thus not homosexuality, but rather the threat of sexual or physical assault or the lack of hospitality to these unknown guests. Homosexuality is not shown as the norm in any of the societies in Genesis or Judges, thus it could not be regarded as the reasons for God's wrath. The threat of sexual assault can be seen as a demonstration of power over outsiders represented by the angels or the foreign man in Judges rather than a loving sexual act.

The major Christian and Jewish teachings do not view the sins of Sodom and Gomorrah as referring to homosexuality, and this has only been adopted by extremely small sects as official church teaching. But these ideas have somehow permeated into popular culture. This has even inspired the term *sodomy* to refer to any form of nonreproductive sex, especially anal sex.

The Jewish faith sees the crimes of Sodom and Gomorrah as cruelty, a lack of hospitality, economic crimes, greed, blasphemy and violence.

Many progressive Christian interpretations show that there might not even have been a sexual connotation to the exchange with Lot, as the word *yada*, used by the townsmen to explain that they want to "know" the angels, only has a sexual connotation in about one percent of uses in the Bible. This might just have been a reference to the angels being seen as foreigners and the townspeople's desire to have access to them and assault them. Similar sins as those referred to in the Jewish faith are usually seen as the true sins of Sodom and Gomorrah in most major Christian interpretations.

Considering the evidence, it is widely accepted that these stories have nothing to do with homosexuality, and loving gay relationships were surely not the reason for the destruction of these cities, not even in the broadest interpretation.

3. In 1 Corinthians 6: 9-11, Paul the Apostle wrote:

"Know ye not that the unrighteous shall not inherit the kingdom of God? Be not deceived: neither fornicators, nor idolaters, nor adulterers, nor effeminate, nor abusers of themselves with mankind, Nor thieves, nor covetous, nor drunkards, nor revilers, nor extortioners, shall inherit the kingdom of God. And such were some of you: but ye are washed, but ye are sanctified, but ye are justified in the name of the Lord Jesus, and by the Spirit of our God."

This is one of the weakest translations used to attack homosexuality. In some translations they become a lot more clearly targeted, even collapsing the two words into "homosexuals" in order to drive home the force of the mistranslation.

In fact, the two terms have very broad meanings and have become so misrepresented that they are falsely adopted by anti-gay movements.

The first term, often translated as "effeminate", comes from the Greek translation *malakoi* which literally means "soft", and might refer to anything from vanity, laziness, cowardice, vulnerability, decadency or any number of other traits. The connotation was usually linked to a man who does not have traditionally masculine, dominant traits like bravery or stoicism. Thus, men who showed emotion would also have this term applied to them. The word *malakoi* is never used with a sexual connotation anywhere else in the Bible, so there is no reason to believe it is used in that way here.

Some translations also link this term to male prostitutes or the receptive partners in homosexual intercourse since the term can also refer to being "like a woman", although this would be quite a broad translation, unsupported by the remainder of the religious text. Paul refers to many different sins in his list, and it is much more likely, based on the root word, to refer to behavior not fitting of the traditional view of a man. The best translation would probably be "having weak morals".

The second term, *arsenokoitai*, often translated as "abusers of themselves with mankind" is even more of a blurry translation, as this term is extremely rare. In fact, Paul seems to have coined this term himself, as no earlier usages are found. This term almost certainly does not merely refer to homosexuals, as many other words which directly refer to same-sex relations could have been used instead. In the few instances this word was used at the time, it is often understood to be a connection between power and sex, and might best be understood, as in the story of Lot, to refer to sexual abuse or using sex to gain power over or to humiliate others. It might also refer to sexual predators or those who abuse young children sexually. However, since Paul seems to have coined the term, and subsequent uses mostly point back to his list of sins, the meaning of this term is likely lost and will never be clear.

These two very broad translations (or mistranslations) can in no way be taken as irrefutable condemnation of gay people, except by readers who manipulate the texts.

4. **In 1 Timothy 1: 8-11, Paul explains:**

"But we know that the law is good, if a man use it lawfully; Knowing this, that the law is not made for a righteous man, but for the lawless and disobedient, for the ungodly and for sinners, for unholy and profane, for murderers of fathers and murderers of mothers, for manslayers, for whoremongers, for them that defile themselves with mankind, for menstealers, for liars, for perjured persons, and if there be any other thing that is contrary to sound doctrine; According to the glorious gospel of the blessed God, which was committed to my trust."

In 1 Timothy 1, Paul again refers to a single category which has been translated as "homosexuals" or "them that defile themselves with mankind". He also used this term in the Corinthians passage discussed above, namely the Greek translation *arsenokoitai*. This term obviously cannot directly be translated as "homosexuals" as many versions of the Bible do, as the term *homosexual* and the concept of same-sex primary attraction was only conceptualized in the 19th century, and if it were his intention to condemn same-sex relations there were many terms from the period Paul could have used.

We can therefore say with confidence that the term used most likely does not refer to homosexuality, but rather to those who use sex for power or dominance.

5. **In Romans 1: 26-27, Paul again says:**

"For this cause God gave them up unto vile affections: for even their women did change the natural use into that which is against nature: And likewise also the men, leaving the natural use of the woman, burned in their lust one toward another; men with men working that which is unseemly, and receiving in themselves that recompense of their error which was meet."

Now already it seems that the Biblical basis for justifying homophobia, and which has resulted in victimization, pain and suffering for millions of young men who dare love other men, is losing its absoluteness.

In reference to this particular passage, Paul is writing a letter to the Romans about how well they are adhering to Christianity. He explains that there are many who do not worship God but rather worship idols or commit other sins, and because of this they are turned to "unnatural" lusts.

The term "unnatural" here is also very loosely translated, and more accurately would be translated as "uncustomary" or not of the customs of the Jewish or early Christian communities. Paul noticed exploitative same-sex relations such as temple prostitution and other cultish sexual practices within the pagan and Greek societies, and saw these as being against the customs of Jewish teachings, and immediately associated these with idol worship which took place in these societies. Paul was not referring to loving gay relationships in these statements, but specifically to the temple prostitution and other forms of sexual exploitation which were practised at the time.

Paul's background and his cultural context can clearly be seen as informing this passage. Importantly, Paul does not condemn homosexuality outright here, even though he seems to use strong language to show his disdain for some forms of same-sex relations. Rather, he focuses on idol worship as what he sees as a precursor to these "uncustomary" relations.

So where does that leave me and my faith?

When evidence from a number of Biblical scholars is considered, it seems much less likely that the Bible directly condemns homosexuality and loving same-sex relationships.

Many people see the Bible as the clear, direct, literal words of God, merely transcribed by other people. Others, including the majority of Biblical scholars and religious leaders, see it as a historical text, written by many different thinkers, translated from Hebrew to Greek and then to many other languages. These texts are set within a specific context, and they share valuable, important spiritual parables and truths which help people live better lives, find understanding and grow in faith.

Many people see God as an angry, vengeful, cruel ruler, while others see Him as a loving, forgiving, welcoming, accepting presence whose main desire is for people to grow and share joy and fulfilment in this life and the next by living good lives and not harming others.

What we hope is clear from what we've just discussed is that the Bible does not clearly and categorically condemn homosexuals, and the ambiguity of the statements in this section, for some, is sadly enough to sacrifice the love of their gay sons.

While we can't tell you how to engage with your faith, we urge you to reflect on the ambiguous and diminishing evidence of a God that directs hate towards men who happen to love other men. Only you as the parent of a gay son can decide whether the evidence of God's wrath is clear enough for you to be sure that you are really doing God's work by condemning gay people and victimising your son.

You also need to recognize that if your child is religious, he might be wrestling with his own guilt and shame because of how many people use religion to condemn homosexuality. Showing him that God's love is unconditional will give him the emotional and spiritual strength to work through these feelings with courage and honesty.

Ultimately, religions are about God's infinite love, and that should be your approach when engaging with your child. Do some soul-searching and use your own thinking. Remember that it is fallible human beings who have interpreted God's word, used it for hatred and abuse, and condemned gay and lesbian teens to damnation. The recent more permissive attitudes of some Catholic leaders, including the new pope[57], towards homosexuality, and the election of the first gay Anglican bishop[58] in 2003 shows that religious attitudes are not stagnant. Times are changing, and religions are too.

When faced with the choice of sticking to very murky translations on the one hand and accepting and loving your son, you need to decide which course of action most embodies the spirit of your faith and your role as a parent.

Chapter 5: Gay culture: why does my son love Lady Gaga so much?

Is there such a thing as "gay culture"?

Strictly speaking, no. There are many millions of gay people worldwide, and they are just as diverse as straight people. Some of them embrace and celebrate their gay identity, while others are less self-accepting. Some of them feel a real sense of community and togetherness with other gay people, while others dislike or avoid the stereotypical gay culture or gay-friendly spaces due to their own personal preference. People are not all the same, and remembering this is one of the most important ways to engage with your son in his individuality and complexity.

A segment of the gay population has, however, formed a culture in order to show their connection with and celebration of being gay, and many gay people do have similar interests according to research.

Many gay people who embrace gay identity and culture often identify with the symbol of the rainbow to signify the diversity of all people in terms of sexuality and gender, and the rainbow flag is often attached to gay political and social movements, such as the marriage equality movement. Don't be freaked out if you see this on your son's backpack or above his bed; he is merely trying to figure out where he fits in.

There are also certain common interests in gay people linked to gay subcultures and countercultures. These will be explored in this chapter.

You might find that your son engages with these aspects of gay culture, either regularly or sporadically, as a way of discovering himself and his place in the world, or out of genuine interest for the things that are linked with the popular ideas of the gay subculture.

But overall, most gay people do not frequent gay bars or clubs, are not actively involved in gay political or social initiatives, are not promiscuous, and do not automatically embrace all aspects of the very narrow popular conception of "gay culture". Most gay people, just like straight people, have extremely diverse interests and ways of expressing themselves. They just happen to be attracted to the same sex.

While we will address certain aspects of the commonly understood "gay culture" in this chapter, it is important not to stereotype these aspects to all gay people. These ideas about gay culture have become popular and are practised by many gay people, but certainly not all and probably not even most gay people would identify with them. They are only useful in so far as they help you with understanding the types of things your son might show a preference for in the process of discovering himself.

Why do people often refer to the "gay community"?

Due to how painful and marginalising homophobia can be, many gay people are looking for acceptance and equal rights, and many of them rely on other gay people and gay rights movements in order to find a sense of identity and to work towards these social goals. The gay community is a term used to refer to a group of people with similar experiences in the world, but definitely *not* the same experiences. Individual experiences depend on lots of factors, including race, age, social class, and family acceptance.

Sometimes those who are anti-gay will also use the term "gay community" in order to stereotype gay people or demonize them. For example, some people say "the gay community wants to destroy marriage and recruit children" or "the gay community has no morals". There is no such "gay community" out to destroy culture or the world as we know it, and people use these ideas to spread hatred. It's important to be sure of how this term is used when you encounter it.

Gay culture as a subculture

Gay people were often forced into hiding who they were publicly in order to avoid homophobic treatment or attacks, and this led to feeling like outsiders within dominant heterosexual cultures. For this reason, many gay people formed part of a gay subculture, or a culture where they could express their interests, embrace their identity and feel more accepted. When being gay was criminalized in most countries (it is still criminalized in over 70 countries[59]), this subculture usually involved meeting in secluded places and keeping relationships secret. Still, gay spaces like gay-friendly bars or nightclubs were often raided by police and even these small spaces of freedom were under attack.

When political movements to challenge homophobia emerged in some societies, these were linked with a revolution for LGBT people. For example, the 1969 Stonewall riots in New York City were protests against police raids of gay spaces, and signalled the start of the gay liberation movement in the US. For most, this was simply the movement to accept gay people within wider society. Gay culture became preoccupied with celebrating gay identity and legitimizing gay intimacy, and these became the hallmarks of the gay subculture. Many segments of the gay community also fought to legalize homosexuality where it was illegal, for more gay rights and to counter homophobia.

Due to these origins, the popular view of the gay subculture became very sexualized, and many gay activists embraced this aspect of gay culture since it was seen as a symbol of overcoming societal hatred of gay intimacy.

Research also shows that gay men are more prone to creativity[60]. It's been suggested that this is due to their alternative experiences and how they need to internalize a lot of their experiences due to not being able to talk freely about their sexuality. It might also be the result of gay people feeling more accepted in bohemian, artistic spaces, like major cities, where diversity is more accepted. Many gay people thus show an interest in creative expression, such as through fashion, design, dance, theatre, music, and writing. Being unique and different in how they express themselves might be a way of asserting their own identity and individuality when they are often made to hide their sexuality.

Again, these are some of the more visible trends but they do not apply to all gay men.

Gay culture as a counterculture

In contrast to the idea that gay culture is a subculture, some people see it as a counterculture[61]. The distinction might be important as it can shape the way we see ourselves and others. As a result of the rejection which many gay people face in their lives, they often rebel against heterosexual culture in order to claim the legitimacy of their gay identity. This involves reclaiming stereotypes in positive ways, such as expressing a more effeminate side when around other gay people and embracing language styles, terms and cultural practices of popular gay cultures.

This gives rise to practices like drag, which is different from transgenderism. Whereas transgenderism is a gender identity, in drag, dressing as a woman is often seen as a countercultural performance[62] by someone who identifies as male, entertaining people by playing with stereotypes in different and empowering ways. Gay men are able to show their uniqueness and difference and feel the freedom to be as feminine as they like with exaggerated costumes, make-up and singing or lip-synching routines. Very few gay men feel comfortable doing drag themselves, but it is a celebrated part of gay culture and performers can gain large followings.

In line with this idea that we can think about gay culture, gay men often embrace their status as outsiders in order to reclaim power in this status, and they might refer to themselves by terms which previously were hurtful to them, such as queer. They are often attracted to performers who celebrate difference and upset or challenge conventional culture, which is why Lady Gaga or other avant-garde performers are so popular among many gay men.

Gay men also often embrace empowered, androgynous women as role models, especially those who have struggled through adversity and achieved success in their lives. This can be linked to the celebration of gender nonconforming behavior or strength in femininity. They identify with those who have been hurt in love and who feel like outsiders, as well as those who embrace their sexuality, and those who actively voice support for LGBT causes. Gay men also often idolize those who show a flair for glamour, flamboyance or outrageousness in fashion and manner, looking to them as symbols of a counterculture. This is why prominent female artists or media personalities like Madonna, Beyoncé, Diana Ross, Judy Garland, Oprah Winfrey, Barbra Streisand, Cher, Bette Midler, Liza Minnelli, Marilyn Monroe and many others become "gay icons", and many drag artists impersonate them.

This list of common cultural features of course does not apply to all gay people, but could explain at least some of your gay son's new interests that you don't necessarily understand.

Gay people as surrogate families

Even though LGBT youth make up a small minority of the entire youth population (estimated at 3-5%), they make up 40% of the homeless youth population[63] in the United States.

How to Understand and Accept Your Gay Son

The reasons for this should be clear. Many families reject and outcast their LGBT children, or many of these children do not feel comfortable or accepted in their homes, leaving them with nowhere to go but the streets. In our work and research, we have heard devastating stories from many young people who say that being rejected by family and friends made them feel hopeless and feel like they have nowhere to call home or no one with whom to talk.

Due to the high rejection rate by families and friends, and the fact that many gay people have to hide who they are for most of their lives, they can often find a lot of comfort in forming close bonds with other LGBT people. These groups become like surrogate families, helping each other through the coming out process and offering emotional support through challenging times.

No one will understand your child's struggles as well as other LGBT people, so these bonds are very important in self-acceptance. But you can make life a lot easier for your child as well by giving them support in their real family so that they are not left without support or forced to seek it outside. The fact that your son may be embracing a "family" of other gay guys does not undermine the central role that you can still play in his life as a loving parent and stable family core.

Gay Pride

One of the hallmarks of gay culture over the past few decades has been gay pride parades and celebrations across the world. These are places where gay people can feel a sense of visibility, solidarity and empowerment within public spaces, the exact same spaces where they are often forced to hide who they are.

Gay pride parades are often colourful and party-themed, with lots of singing, dancing and empowering, fun music, but there are also more serious elements, such as lots of *PFLAG* members marching along, church organisations showing their support for LGBT causes, and even political posters or groups who show their support for gay rights in countries where being gay is criminalized. This includes the majority of African countries where anti-gay sentiment is extremely strong.

For many gay people, gay pride celebrations, and other gay events like gay film festivals, can be extremely liberating and can help to spread the visibility and acceptance of gay people by including larger communities.

While these festivals are not without their problems, the spirit behind gay pride is meant to be one of inclusivity and celebrating diversity.

Gay spaces

In most parts of the world, there are very few spaces where gay people can be themselves and have fun with or dance with their same-sex partners. Gay bars, restaurants and nightclubs offer spaces where gay people can feel free to express their identity. It must be noted that only a small percentage of gay people enjoy these types of gay spaces, and that they are not for everyone.

While it might be a great experience for your son to enjoy such spaces and to find somewhere where he can be himself when he is old enough, it is important to remember that the same pitfalls do apply to these inclusive spaces as with straight bars and clubs. These include alcohol abuse, drug use and the potential for unsafe sex. In fact, some studies show that gay men are between three[64] and seven times[65] more likely to use illegal drugs than straight people, possibly linked to social pressures or the mental health concerns of *minority stress*. You still need to be just as strict with your gay child as you would be with a straight child, and instil a sense of responsibility and self-worth in him so that he does not succumb to these dangerous elements. If he gets involved with the local gay club scene, you can be equally supportive and realistic with him about what he might encounter.

It is undoubtable, both from[66] research[67] and in our experiences, that accepting, supportive home environments generally lead to much lower rates of risky sexual behavior, substance abuse or mental health issues, so you can do your part to protect your child by accepting and loving them.

Gay relationships and dating

Some popular myths about gay relationships are that they are unstable, short-lived or that the partners are always unfaithful. In fact, while research, especially from more than a decade ago or in repressed communities, does show some erratic relationship patterns, there are very few differences between gay and straight relationships[68]. In addition, gaps are narrowing as homosexuality and gay marriage are legalized and accepted in many parts of the world. This could be because there is less stress on relationships now, as they no longer hide from society's disapproval.

All relationships are fragile and challenging, and it will all depend on how much self-acceptance both partners have, their personalities and not to mention support from family and friends. If one or more factors are out of place, relationships will almost always suffer or be unhappy. Most studies done on gay dating and relationships are very limited and not representative. So it's hard to draw any meaningful comparisons; after all, we simply don't know the number of gay men out there and what each relationship looks like. But we've found that the vast majority of gay men we've worked with are only looking for love, stability and a partner to share their lives with. Many of them are just looking in all the wrong places since there have traditionally been so few opportunities to meet other gay people.

Gay dating can involve using online dating sites or phone applications since it is very difficult to simply approach someone in public who you might find attractive (they might be straight or even anti-gay, which could lead to embarrassment or even violence). Similarly, there are very few gay spaces, and the majority of gay people do not frequent these spaces. Due to these limited opportunities, these gay websites have become popular for meeting new people. There are a wide variety of these sites available, some of them largely for finding friends or dating partners. Others are very sexualized and mostly used for hook-ups. Chances are your son will at least try one of these sites in order to meet other gay guys and while this may unsettle you, the most important thing you can do is establish a relationship of honesty and trust with your son.

When he is of age, he will need someone that he trusts and loves to encourage a healthy understanding of sex and explain to him that real connection rarely comes from hook-ups. There is no reason why you can't give him the same speech that you would give to his straight brother or sister: while some forms of sex can be fulfilling, beautiful and fun, there is also the chance that other people can use you only for your body, and superficial sexual encounters can be damaging for your self-esteem, dangerous for the risk of HIV and other STIs, and rarely lead to the meaningful bonds that most people seek. It is much more likely that your son wants a real meaningful emotional connection than just lots of sex. You might want to encourage your son to try dating sites for long-term connections. You could even suggest that he find gay pen pals if he is looking for a meaningful connection.

You can assume that your son will probably go through the same tumultuous dating patterns that straight young people go through, either finding a long-term partner at a young age or going through years of dating, heartbreak, and falling in and out of love just like any young person. Now many parents report feeling very uncomfortable when their gay son first brings a person with whom they are in a relationship with home to meet the family. But reacting negatively to this moment is such a lost opportunity to share in your son's personal life and to celebrate the relationship of trust and respect that he obviously feels with you.

Your approach should be to treat it just like any other relationship. Depending on the personalities of your son and the partner he finds, they might be perfectly suited to have a healthy, monogamous long-term relationship as many gay young people these days do. We've witnessed many stable, loving gay relationships in our work, and we are in a stable, loving relationship ourselves. In fact, recent polls show that the majority of single gay and lesbian people <u>do want to get married</u>[69].

Being in the closet

This refers to the time before a gay person tells other people that he is gay, or before they are willing to accept that they are gay. The metaphor is used to show that the gay person is not ready to reveal his identity to other people yet, or might have actively decided to hide who he is.

Many gay people spend years in the closet, but, depending on the environment you create at home or the general openness of your community, your son might feel comfortable coming out a lot sooner and beginning to accept himself.

Coming out

Coming out of the closet is not a once-off thing. It is usually a very long process for a gay person.

For many gay people, coming out is an extremely transformative process. It can either come with a great sense of relief as the gay person is finally able to be himself and to tell others about it, or it can be very hard if family and friends reject him.

Some people are so afraid of rejection that they never come out and spend their entire lives hiding who they are. Some end up marrying opposite-sex partners but cheating on them with same-sex encounters and live a lonely life of emotional deprivation.

The first step in coming out is usually some measure of accepting the fact that one is gay. A gay person might develop feelings for another person of the same sex and feel very anxious about this for a long time. Many people report <u>trying to change</u>[70] themselves through prayer or to try and focus on making themselves attracted to the opposite sex throughout adolescence, but failing to do so. You know by now that it is not possible to change or choose your sexual identity.

Once they have accepted that they are gay, people will often first tell a close friend or someone else they can trust.

How to Understand and Accept Your Gay Son

Eventually, as they learn to truly gain self-acceptance, they will engage in more difficult coming-out moments, such as disclosing a relationship in the work environment, or telling their families where rejection has more serious consequences. You can find some coming out videos on YouTube. Many of these videos show positive outcomes to coming out, but there are some extremely negative and even violent ones where gay people are rejected by their families, so be cautioned. These will show you how scary the coming out process can be, and why your son might have taken a long time to come out to you.

Some people might engage in what is known as *covering*. This is when they try to hide aspects of their personality - such as their interests or attractions - or try to deepen their voices or change the way they walk in order to try and hide the fact that they are gay.

Some people might also try to date someone of the opposite sex even when they know that they are attracted to the same sex, something commonly known as *bearding*. The *beard* is the opposite-sex partner who is used to cover the fact that the person is really gay, often without knowing that they are the beard.

There are those people who never come out at all and who live their entire lives denying that they are gay. This is often linked with severe personal distress[71] and even resentment of their opposite-sex partners.

These different aspects of gay culture might give you some insight into the world of your son as he learns to accept himself. Later, we provide you with some scripted guidelines to help you discuss various topics with him and to show him your understanding and acceptance.

Chapter 6: I'm not supposed to ask this, but...

Are gay people destined for a lonely, sad life?

Not at all - dependent on a few factors.

Gay people from previous generations were much less likely to have children (biological or adopted) to spend time with them later in life. They were also much more likely to suffer the rejection of family members as attitudes were far less accepting.

These factors led to recent studies[72] showing that gay and bisexual people over 55 have far less contact with family members than their straight counterparts.

There is also a much smaller gay dating pool, leading many older people to still be single late in life.

But as times are changing, there are also major shifts in gay relationships.

Due to gay marriage being legalized in many parts of the world, couples now have more stability in relationships and more social acceptance, leading to healthier, longer lasting bonds. (In fact, gay couples are currently still less likely to divorce[73] than straight couples, but this will probably change as same-sex relationships become less of a novelty). Internet dating now also creates a wider dating pool.

Families are also more accepting of gay relatives, and no longer cut off contact with them at the same rates in developing nations.

There is nothing inherently lonely about being gay, but the way society treats gay people could have an impact on making life easier or harder for them.

Do older gay men recruit younger children to be gay?

Absolutely not! This is one example of a harmful myth that is often spread by social conservatives as fact. Much scientific research has been done to discover the 'origin' or 'causes' of homosexuality, and none of this research has yielded any findings that suggest that gay people recruit straight people to be gay. Some sources point to the origin of this myth as certain groups claiming that since homosexual men cannot reproduce, they will naturally then focus their efforts on 'recruiting' children into the 'homosexual lifestyle'. The myth could also be based on misinformation about how human sexuality functions, or the idea that it is a "choice" to be gay.

This is an especially pernicious myth, as it makes another insidious implication: that of gay men being pedophiles. For men to 'recruit' children, it heavily implies that these men molest children in some way. This further serves to demonize gay men and is a strategy to justify homophobia.

If being gay is a part of someone's identity, this is who they are, and no one else can "recruit" them to be that way. Your son probably has had much more interaction with straight people in his life than gay people, but he was not "recruited" to be straight, and like many gay people might even have tried to force himself to be straight, but sexuality and sexual identity cannot be chosen or engineered in this way.

Is being gay equivalent to or related to pedophilia?

Being gay means being attracted to people of the same sex. There are no violent, antisocial, harmful or destructive tendencies attached to this sexual identity. Most gay people seek to form loving bonds with consenting partners, and in their adulthood they do not have sexual attraction to children but rather to other consenting adults, just like straight people.

Being a pedophile means being attracted to young children. Those who act on these feelings are child molesters because children cannot legally give consent to sexual relations and are not psychologically prepared or sexually advanced enough to engage in adult sexual activities. Child molestation is extremely damaging for children.

Child molestation has nothing to do with homosexuality. Most child molesters identify as straight[74], and there is no evidence linking homosexuality to a higher prevalence of child molestation.

People try and equate the two categories in order to link homosexuality with sexual deviance and destructive sexual patterns. But really, they have nothing to do with one another.

But they can't have kids! Doesn't that make it unnatural?

While it is true that two men cannot reproduce, this is not a factor that only applies to gay men. There are heterosexual people who cannot reproduce for biological or genetic reasons. Surely most heterosexual couples also have sex for reasons other than just reproducing. Are their relationships also "unnatural"? Is their love less legitimate than couples who can procreate?

It is also useful to consider the reasons why people have sex. Some common reasons include, but are not limited to:

- sex is fun
- sex is an expression of physical intimacy
- sex is an expression of emotional intimacy
- sex is a form of stress relief
- sex is an expression of being in love
- sex cements a commitment in one's relationship

So we can see that there are many reasons why people are intimate. None of the reasons above are more valid than the others. In previous times, heterosexual marital sex used to be the only socially acceptable form of sex. But that is not the case anymore. Many heterosexual couples move in together without being married. Why do you think the same degree of judgment and scorn is not leveled at these people who also violate conservative sexual norms? If marital sexual intercourse for the purpose of reproduction is the only acceptable form of sexual intercourse, what about postmenopausal women who are sexually active? Or men with extremely low sperm counts?

While it is certainly true that people are not animals, homosexual behavior is present in over 450 animal species[75] - and those are only the recorded homosexual behaviors that have been observed to date. While people certainly operate on much more sophisticated and advanced levels of spiritual, cognitive, sexual, and psychological functioning, we are at core an animal species with biological drives. The fact that so many different species participate in same-sex activities bolsters the claim that homosexuality is not "unnatural".

Are there "men" and "women" in gay relationships, and which role does my son take?

Generally speaking, men are gay because they are attracted to other men, and thus neither partner takes the role of a woman and neither is required to. While there is a broad spectrum of sexual preferences, these other preferences on the LGBTQIA range usually do not go along with being gay, and you can anticipate that your gay son is a man who still identifies as a man and is attracted to other men who still identify as men. If he tells you differently, hear him out, but don't assume that all relationships need to fit the model of one "man" and one "woman".

What you might be curious about are the dynamics of household responsibilities, power relations, sex roles, and how he and his partner have masculine or feminine traits. These vary from relationship to relationship, just like they do in straight relationships, and as long as he is in a functional partnership these aspects should not really concern you.

Don't try to figure out who is the "man" or "woman", and don't comment on it. These types of ideas can be embarrassing and limiting, and demonstrate a lack of understanding for what it means to be gay and what it means to be a multifaceted person. You might still be trying to see your child in terms of what applies to straight relationships, but these labels are not applicable to gay relationships.

Is it okay to wonder about or ask about who is the "top" or the "bottom" in my son's relationship?

We'll answer this because it's a question that some parents do ask their sons or wonder about, but if this explicit talk makes you uncomfortable, please do skip this answer.

The "top" refers to the active or penetrating sexual partner, and the "bottom" refers to the receptive partner during anal intercourse.

While you might be curious about gay sex, in part because it goes against conventions for men to be receptive sexual partners, it must be clear that it is *very* inappropriate to ask about what he does in bed. Your interest in his bedroom activities should surely be limited to making sure that he is being safe. Would you ask your straight child about what he or she does in bed?

But gay men aren't real men, are they?

Gay men are "real" men just as much as straight men are "real" men. This is because they identify as men.

What might lead people to think that gay men aren't real men is the issue of heterosexism. Society considers the only legitimate sexuality to be heterosexuality, because this is what our social institutions might be telling us. But this is simply a perspective. There is nothing that constitutes a "real" man. All people have traits which might be traditionally masculine or feminine, but it is important to note that these are only based on *tradition* and not on biology. Our ideas of gender are created by society, and are known as *social constructs*, and are not essential truths based on science or reason.

For example, picture a man who is very affectionate and nurturing with his children. Is he a real man? What if he is a stay-at home dad? Or a man who cries when he feels sad? What about a man who spends a lot of time on his appearance? Or a man who enjoys wearing pink: is he a real man?

These ideas were very far-fetched for men only a few years ago, but now they are commonplace. And if there is a change in society, the ideas change as well. Some ideas of gender even differ greatly from one society to the next. For example, in parts of Asia, Africa and many Arab countries, straight men hold hands in public as a sign of friendship. In many parts of Europe, straight men also kiss each other's cheeks in greeting. This does not make them any less masculine in these societies, even though it would be frowned upon in some parts of the world.

So your son is a "real man" if he identifies as a man, and any other factors don't matter.

Grant Andrews & Malan van der Walt

Will a child be at a disadvantage by having two same-sex parents?

Absolutely not. Various studies have been conducted on this topic. There is almost <u>unanimous agreement</u>[76] within social science that same-sex parents are just as good as opposite-sex parents, as well as the consistent support for gay and lesbian parenting by all major US organisations which deal with children's welfare, including the American Academy of Pediatrics. All of these groups and respected thinkers confirm that there is no difference in outcomes for children of same-sex and opposite-sex parents. In fact, a number of studies show that the children of same-sex parents might be <u>better adjusted</u>[77] in certain fields such as general health, gender parity and family cohesion than the general population. This is possibly due to most same-sex parents having to struggle for longer in order to adopt and mostly choosing to be parents versus unplanned pregnancies in heterosexual relationships.

The major predictor of a healthy, well-adjusted child in gay or straight households is the loving, supportive bond between parent and child. This factor has a much greater impact on the child's wellbeing than whether the parents are opposite- or same-sex. This does not mean that gay people can't be bad parents, but it does mean that they are not more likely to be bad parents than straight people.

How to Understand and Accept Your Gay Son

The best research tells us this: if your son and his partner are loving, attentive parents who provide well for their children, their children will probably grow up to be well-adjusted, successful adults, just like with straight couples.

Grant Andrews & Malan van der Walt

Accepting Your Gay Son

With some useful scripts to use for those challenging conversations

I don't think I can ever accept my son, and it makes me feel terrible that our relationship is so damaged.

Many parents feel this way initially. It is important to remember that *you are not alone* in feeling this way. There are support groups, church groups, PFLAG chapters, gay-straight alliances and other organisations that are filled with people struggling to accept their gay friends and family members.

The reason is that we have all been exposed to so many negative messages about gay people and being gay. We've been told that they are going to hell. We've been told that gay people are hateful. We've been shown negative stereotypes. They might offend many people's ideas about gender norms, and seem strange, different and deviant. You might have heard that they are recruiting children, that they are pedophiles, that it is a choice. Even if you don't believe these untrue things about gay people, the perpetual negative messages have filtered into all of our minds, and we have adopted some of them unknowingly.

Initially it might be incredibly tough to accept that your son is gay, but the vast majority of parents, if they make the effort, do reach a point of acceptance and can rebuild their relationship with their sons if it has been damaged.

Your first step is to overcome your own prejudices and to allow yourself to see the fact that gay people are just normal people with just as wide a range of interests and personalities as straight people. Once you realize that gay people are just like everyone else, it will help you to overcome your knee-jerk reaction to fear or hate them. Some steps for getting to this point are given later in this section.

You also need to start making peace around the conflict between homosexuality and religion. Hopefully Chapter 4 of the previous section will have helped you a bit in this process, but there are many church groups that offer information and support. Try and find one in your area if you still have spiritual concerns about your son being gay.

Give yourself permission to feel all of the feelings that you are feeling, and then remember that living a life of love and sharing a strong relationship with your son, and keeping him healthy and happy, should be your main priorities. Condemning him or resenting him will not help either of you.

I've done the work and soul-searching, and I'm ready to accept my son. Now what?

As you have worked through the previous section of the book, *Understanding your Gay Son*, you should now feel that you have built a greater understanding of what it means to be gay, and what it does not mean to be gay. You should now feel ready to approach your gay son, and to have one of several conversations with him wherein you learn what it means to accept him unconditionally, and to love him without reservation.

What is of great importance is that you infuse your conversations to follow with love, care, compassion, and empathy.

I think that my son is gay but he hasn't spoken to me about it. What should I do?

If your feeling that your son is gay turns out to be true, you are in a somewhat difficult position. We suspect that you are accepting of people that belong to a sexual minority, but you don't want to impose your thoughts about your son possibly being gay onto him, for fear of alienating him, or even catching him by surprise should you be wrong, which will probably lead to both of you feeling embarrassed.

Some people argue that it is better to wait for your son to approach you first. Some family members of gay men have even reported that they felt it better for the son to approach them before they approach him. This might be because they feel it is not their place to impose their suspicions on him, and that it is better to wait for him until he is ready.

However, what is lost in this thinking process, is the fact that the son is left dealing with an identity crisis that oftentimes feels overwhelming and even insurmountable, and that by not making it clear that you would be accepting of a gay son, he is deprived of an invaluable support base in the form of his caregiver. It is our belief that many gay teenagers, for example, would have felt more comfortable coming to terms with their sexuality if their parents communicated to them in no uncertain terms that they would be accepting of a gay child.

Communicating to your son directly and indirectly about what you think he might be going through could be a better move in the short and long term. If he is gay, but hasn't approached you to reveal this part of himself, all of our research and personal experience suggests that hiding this important part of himself is a great source of anxiety[78] for him. We are sure that at this stage, if you have worked through the previous section of the book, you understand more about homosexuality, and hopefully you have even settled some of your concerns regarding it. If this is indeed the case, we would like to encourage you to create a safe and welcoming atmosphere for your son. Here are some ways to modify your environment to achieve this effect:

1. If you find a gay-positive article in a newspaper, magazine, or even book, leave it lying in a room in the house frequented by your son. This could be the kitchen or living room. Your son will no doubt notice it and wonder who has been perusing this kind of material.

2. Comment positively on gay-related news and events. Perhaps there is a section on the news dealing with gay and human rights: be sure to say something that indicates your approval of gay and human rights. Consider the following:

I see that gay marriage has become legalized in even more states now. I find it so encouraging that our nation is moving in a direction of greater equality and freedom for all. I think people should be given the right to be with and marry whomever they like. What do you think?

This is an important move on your part, and you are conveying a lot of important information here. Firstly, you are demonstrating an awareness of the plight of LGBT people. Secondly, you are letting your son know that your attitude regarding gay people has changed. Perhaps you have made an anti-gay statement in the presence of your son some time in the past that you can possibly not even recall. But we can assure you that your son remembers this comment, and it probably hurt him deeply. Thirdly, by saying something similar to our suggested script, you are laying the groundwork for your son to approach you.

3. Should you be in the presence of somebody that says something homophobic, and your son is within earshot, you have now been presented with a golden opportunity to demonstrate your unequivocal support for gay rights. Your son will no doubt take note that you are practising what you are preaching: you are not only supportive of gay people in a one-on-one conversation with your son, but you are going the extra mile and possibly making yourself vulnerable by being a vocal supporter of gay rights. You could use the following script in addressing homophobia when you encounter it:

What you have just said is homophobic. It is probably based on not having met gay people before (at least that you're aware of), or relying on outdated ideas of what it means to be gay, and whether it is right or wrong. However, I want you to know that your homophobia is damaging and offensive, and I would like you to reconsider before you say things that are hurtful and damning to people who do not deserve such treatment. Thank you for listening to me.

Finally, you can consider approaching your son. Throughout a few well-paced moments over a month or two, you have started laying the groundwork and done some important work to make your son feel safe and welcomed if he should choose to come out to you. If your efforts have not paid off in the sense that he does come out to you, do not be discouraged. We can guarantee you that he has taken note of your efforts and is already in a better place. For his own personal reasons, he simply might not be ready yet. If he is religious, he might be waging an internal struggle with his religion. Perhaps he is receiving negative feedback from peers or teachers about homosexuality. These are factors that, until he comes to you, are beyond your control.

However, perhaps as a last sign of good faith that you are on his side at all times, you can consider saying the following:

I want you to know that I love you and want you to be happy. This is very important to me. I love you regardless of who and what you are. In fact, should I ever learn something new about you, I would probably love you even more, because I would know you better than I did before. I want you to know that I will always be here for you if there is anything you want to tell me.

Even if your thoughts about your son's sexuality have been wrong, and he is straight, you have just created a moment between yourself and your son that will instil a lot of trust: a true bonding moment. And you have demonstrated to him that you are open and welcoming to all people. This will make him feel more secure in approaching you in the future about a time where he is struggling to fit into mainstream society for some reason.

My son just caught me off guard and told me he is gay! How do I react?

If you are in the privileged position of having your son approach you personally to reveal this highly personal part of himself, he is also communicating to you that he needs your trust and unconditional acceptance. He has therefore placed you in a position where you can prove your trust, love, acceptance, and willingness to understand. It is not widely reported in the mainstream media, but many LGBT teens are thrown out of their homes once their parents discover their sexual orientation or sexual identity. They are left with no economic recourse. Again, depression might become a big problem.

It is our genuine hope that you will continue to provide a home for your child. However, a common fear among young gay men is that they will be rejected and thrown out of their family home. It is therefore important that you reassure your son that you feel honored that he has shared this intimate part of himself, and that he is safe and welcome at all times in your home. Here is a suggestion of what you might say:

I feel really happy and trusted by you telling me that you are gay. I know that this must have been hard for you, and I commend your courage and bravery. You are my son, and I love you regardless of who you love.

If your son comes out to you at a time that you are not that familiar with what it means to be gay, and would still like to explore your feelings and understanding of homosexuality, you could say the following:

While I am grateful that you told me you are gay, I need some time to process this. Please know that I am not rejecting you. I just need to talk to people, do some research, and ask for other people's advice. I know that being gay is not always easy, and I am concerned about your health and safety, but maybe we can research some of my questions together.

It can be enormously comforting and validating to your child for you to make a concerted effort to broaden and improve your understanding of homosexuality. There is nothing wrong with being confused about gay people; the mistake to make would be to rely on your untested assumptions about gay men and for that to inform your opinion of homosexuality. Try to take a broader view of homosexuality. Consider what you have learned about what the experts have to say. Look up a PFLAG organisation.

It is, however, also important not to pressure yourself into being a supermom or superdad. This is a new and possibly frightening journey that you are embarking on with your son, and it would be unfair on you to have others expect you to not make a single misstep. Do your homework, stay informed, talk to people you trust and respect, and form as holistic a view on homosexuality as you can. Also, be gentle on yourself. Allow yourself some time to process the conflicting and overwhelming emotions you are feeling. If you sense that your son is not understanding your own process of understanding and accepting him, you could consider telling him the following:

I need you to honor my process as well. Please bear in mind that it took years of conditioning for me to have formed my current ideas about gay men. I acknowledge that I may need to revisit some of these assumptions and to work on them a little bit. But it will take time, and I am going to ask you to be patient. Remember that it must have taken you a considerable amount of time to reach your current place of self-acceptance, and it will take me some time and work to make my peace with this.

Grant Andrews & Malan van der Walt

I feel uncomfortable with the thought of my son being with another guy. How do I overcome this discomfort?

In comparison with heterosexual relationships, homosexual male relationships are dramatically underrepresented in media and in everyday life. As a whole, the average media consumer is not exposed to depictions of homosexual attraction, with the result that its actual occurrence is noted by the viewer, and often frowned upon. It brings to mind the old, overused homophobic mantra that "gays shouldn't flaunt it".

Of course, what the speaker of such a comment fails to realize, is that, per his definition, heterosexual people 'flaunt' their heterosexuality on a near constant basis.

The constant sexualisation of women in all forms of media, using sex to sell products, is an example of this. One is constantly exposed to images of women in suggestive poses. To appeal to the heterosexual man, the woman is wearing little clothing, arches her back, leans over to provide an ample view of her cleavage, and pouts her heavily made up lips. All of this sexualized, suggestive body language that we are so constantly exposed to is an example of *heterosexism*. In this case, there is again the assumption that heterosexuality is the exclusive norm, that it is normal and right, and that deviations from heterosexuality are objectionable, often on moral grounds.

Another factor in your discomfort might be the fact that there are so many negative words about gay people. There are dozens upon dozens of hurtful, homophobic epithets to refer to your son. In fact, should you do a quick Google search to compare the number of anti-gay terms with the amount of anti-straight terms, you will find that there are almost no terms used to describe heterosexuality in a demeaning manner. Of course, we are not advocating for more anti-straight terms to be invented; rather, we are making the case that heterosexism (see Chapter 6) is so entrenched in our ways of thinking and doing, that its effects are rarely questioned or critically examined. This abundance of hurtful, homophobic terminology, so casually uttered by many, is likely to increase your discomfort with homosexuality.

All of this has the effect of making homosexuality invisible. Gay men are constantly exposed to heterosexism, which in turn sustains homophobia. The fear of homophobic attacks prevents many gay men from showing affection to their partners. Soon, we find ourselves dealing with a negative feedback loop. The more pressure heterosexism applies on gay men to not be publicly affectionate with their partners, the more heterosexual people are denied the opportunity to see normal, inoffensive, acceptable displays of affection between gay men. All of these processes make it seem like gay men's affection for one another is wrong or immoral. How can one become accustomed to something if you are never permitted to see it firsthand?

What we are trying to say, is that your aversion to seeing your son being affectionate with another guy is not your fault. Lack of exposure and the novelty of seeing two men being intimate with each other can even be seen as a natural reaction, at least for the time being, because it is so taboo. There is no point in denying that you are still uncomfortable with the sight of two men being together.

However, your journey should not end at this stage. There are steps you can take to increase your comfort level with two men showing affection for one another. By doing this, you will be demonstrating to your son that you accept him wholeheartedly and without reservation.

The steps to take are quite simple. If you are uncomfortable with the visual depiction two gay men together, such as holding hands or kissing, consider nonvisual sources to gradually decrease the novelty factor. You can do some research and read short stories depicting gay men who might enjoy a strong emotional connection, which you are more likely to identify with.

As discussed elsewhere in this book, the sexuality of LGBT persons is often a point of great interest in media depictions. You should therefore tread carefully when seeking to make yourself comfortable with depictions of homosexuality, especially if you are going to make use of the Internet.

Below you can find some sources to aid you in your journey towards accepting homosexuality. To aid you in your important goal of becoming more comfortable with homosexuality, consider the following sources:

Justin Richardson, *And Tango Makes Three*[79]

This would be for those who are very much in the beginning stages of exposing themselves to favourable depictions of homosexuality, and do not feel ready to see two men showing affection. This charming little book tells the story of a male penguin couple who would like to become parents. Ironically, it does a wonderful job of humanising the plight of gay men: a simple desire to become a parent can easily become beset by many obstacles, including the legal and biological challenges. Allow yourself to read the story, and in the interest of strengthening your relationship with your son, imagine how he might be feeling as a gay man who has additional challenges to overcome in a quest to becoming a parent. This will serve as a reminder as to why you are learning more about homosexuality: it is to cement your loving and supportive relationship with your son.

Grant Andrews & Malan van der Walt

Images of loving gay couples[80]

This source contains beautiful images of same-sex love. They are of high quality, the composure is excellent, and the lighting is impeccable - most photographers would appreciate the standard of work here. In these images, you will simply be offered the opportunity to be exposed to homosexuality in the same situational contexts that you are repeatedly exposed to heterosexuality.

Furthermore, we can recommend turning to YouTube to watch stories of gay couples as depicted in dramas. DISCLAIMER: We do not advocate the viewing of online material which is protected by copyright. It is up to you to determine what the relevant laws are as it pertains to the legality of viewing YouTube videos.

That said, we would recommend viewing the story of Will and Sonny, on Days of Our Lives. We like this story as it sensitively portrays the anguish faced by Will as he struggles with his sexuality. His coming out was done with grace and no unnecessary gimmicks, and his love story with Sonny is sweet and develops at a gradual, realistic pace, which allows you to root for them.

Additionally, the story of Christian and Syed on EastEnders offers another beautiful love story, with the added element of family rejection and the anguish which this causes Syed.

Now, it might just be that you are not ready to see your son with his boyfriend. While we are sure that you are uncomfortable with the thought of asking your son to suppress his natural instinct to perhaps hold his boyfriend's hand, or to make similar affectionate gestures, we think it is also fair and reasonable to ask him to respect your current position. However, this should come with the caveat that you commit yourself to stretching your comfort zone to include seeing your son show affection with his boyfriend. After all, this is a process for you too, and it's okay for you to take it slowly, so long as you keep pushing yourself forward. If you would like to tell your son that you are not ready to meet his boyfriend, you can consider saying the following:

While I am very happy that you have found someone that seems to be making you happy, and I appreciate that you would like to introduce him to me, I am not yet ready. This is not because I want to deny you your happiness, or because I want to discourage you from seeing him. And it is very important to me that you not think I am ashamed of you in any way. But this is new to me, and I feel a little bit overwhelmed. I need some time to do some internal work. I look forward to meeting him in the near future and please tell him I say hello.

Shame can be a very damaging emotion. It thrives on guilt, secrecy, and self-loathing, and contributes to a negative emotional state overall. It is therefore imperative that you assure your son you are not ashamed of him. The above script should make it clear that you are committed to being there for him 100%, and that includes meeting and getting to know his boyfriend when you are ready. But you are also allowed a timeline for these events to occur, and it would be unfair for anybody to expect you to see your son with his boyfriend too soon after you find out he is gay. In the meanwhile, make sure that you regularly ask your son how his boyfriend is doing, ask him about his likes and dislikes, provide a friendly and attentive ear if he would like to discuss his relationship, and endeavor to be as supportive and emotionally present as possible. This will demonstrate to your son that you are making a concerted effort to become comfortable with the idea of your son being in a same-sex relationship. Your son will notice your effort and likely be more patient in giving you time to meet his boyfriend.

How to Understand and Accept Your Gay Son

What NOT to say to your son when you find out he is gay

While you might initially be surprised, shocked, angry or even embarrassed when your son tells you he is gay, there are some reactions that can be extremely damaging for him and for your relationship. Saying the wrong thing during this sensitive time might make your son feel ashamed of himself, or lead to him thinking that you no longer love or support him. Below is a list of what *not* to say when your son comes out to you, and reasons why these phrases or ideas might be harmful.

"It is just a phase."

You will know from the first few chapters of this book that being gay is not a phase, and is a part of someone's identity, just like being straight is. While it does happen with a few people that same-sex attraction or relationships are either specific to one person or are part of sexual exploration before a heterosexual relationship is started (many heterosexual people state that they have had some form of same-sex sexual activity in their lives), this is not the case for people who identify as gay, where the primary attraction is for the same sex. Even if your son simply tells you that he finds another guy attractive, you should accept that this might be a part of his way of telling you that he is gay, and treat it as such without the expectation that it will go away. Otherwise, your son might never feel safe enough to share the truth about himself with you.

Here is a suggestion of what you can say instead if you still need clarity on his sexuality:

Thank you for confiding in me. I can imagine it must have been difficult for you, and I value your trust in me and your faith in our relationship. For my own sake, I need some more clarity. Are you absolutely sure that you are gay? Have you felt this way for a long time? Are you comfortable being gay or are you still uncertain?

We believe such questions are fair to ask. If framed in a sensitive and understanding way, and not presented in a doubting, disbelieving style, your son shouldn't take too much offense at being asked this. These are questions that we have been presented with as well, and we understood where it came from, and felt comfortable affirming our truth. We believe the same will be true for your son if he is at a place of self-acceptance. Once he confirms his sexuality, continue doing your work in accepting this truth about him, and do not doubt it. You will risk damaging your relationship and the trust he has in you if you do.

"I can't believe you didn't tell me first."

The coming out process is very sensitive and your son might feel extremely vulnerable and fear rejection. Due to this he might first try telling someone where the stakes are not quite as high, such as a friend, where rejection is less severe than with a parent. You should communicate that you are grateful for your son's honesty, and not try to shame him for not feeling comfortable to talk with you sooner. If you are hurt that he didn't come to you first, think back to a time in your life where you had a painful secret that you felt you needed to keep from your own parents. Consider the fact that if you are the last person he told, it might mean that your acceptance of him is of the utmost importance to him. It is understandable if you feel hurt that he may be hesitant to tell you intimate things about himself, but this can also be seen as a sign of seeking independence and forming his own identity independent of his parents' approval. Instead of feeling resentful of being the last person to be in the know, rather assure him that he can tell you anything, even if he thinks you might disapprove.

"It is abnormal."

This message will very likely add to a sense of self-hatred in your child. He will see himself as flawed, broken or unacceptable. You should focus your messages on making him feel safe and loved, not judged or displeasing. And while homosexuality might fall out of the norm, being 'abnormal' is very different from being 'out of the norm'. Abnormal implies an inherent deficiency. And as discussed before, research supports the idea that homosexuality is a perfectly normal sexual orientation.

"You just have to pray harder."

Many people use a religious foundation in order to try and fight their sexual identity, but this has not been shown to work. You cannot "pray away the gay," no matter how hard you try. In fact, many leaders of religious groups who try and use faith-based reparative therapies actually claim that they were merely hiding their sexuality and that prayer did not cure them, such as the founders of the group Exodus International, and many others whose stories you can view in the video here[81]. This message makes being gay your son's "fault" because he is not practising his faith in the right way, but the truth is that his sexual identity is not going to change and he will merely be denying who he is and never be able to fall in love like he wants to. Trying to change one's sexual orientation in the misguided belief that prayer can achieve this leads to anxiety, depression, and suicidal ideation, if not suicide attempts. If your son is religious, telling him to pray harder will possibly make him feel out of touch with his religion and with God, and will induce guilt and shame. And guilt and shame will not make your son become attracted to women.

"Don't tell anybody about this."

This message will shroud his identity in secrecy and shame, making it seem like something you are embarrassed about. In order to support his good mental health, honest reflection and his sense of self-worth, you need to make it clear that you are proud of him and who he is. If you don't feel that way immediately, try to open the conversation with him instead of merely telling him to keep it a secret. Consider saying the following:

Thank you for telling me about this. I can imagine that it was hard for you to do. I need to process this and collect my own thoughts before I am able to discuss this or deal with this with people we know. I am not ashamed of you, and love you unconditionally, but please give me some time to understand this privately before expecting me to talk about this openly.

"It is your choice."

We trust that by now, you know that being gay is not a choice. Saying this makes it seem like your child is trying wilfully to defy you, your church or society at large that might still be homophobic and think that being gay is wrong. It is his identity, not his choice, and all of your messages to him should acknowledge this fact.

"I will never accept the fact that you are gay."

This line immediately creates a rift between you and your son. You close off the chance for communication and demonstrate your unwillingness to hear what he has to say. Chances are, just like millions of other parents who initially thought they would not be able to accept their LGBT child, you will change your mind in future and your heart will open to accepting your child's identity. Don't damage your relationship by rejecting him at the start. These are words that he is likely to remember for the rest of his life. If you feel strongly that you cannot deal with this information at present, instead of making such a damning statement, you can ask your son to give you some time to collect your thoughts, and ask him not to expect too much of you. Importantly, affirm that you love him no matter what, and that you are not rejecting him, but that you just need some time to understand what he said.

I've already said some of these damaging things. What now?

The best thing that you can do is to confront it head-on. Don't just try to pretend that you did not say what you said before, but rather acknowledge it, admit that it was a mistake, apologize and then let your son know that you did not mean to cause the damage that you might have caused. Oftentimes LGBT youth leave their home when they feel rejected by their parents, or they are thrown out. If this is the case with your son, you could consider writing him a letter as well. If you made one of these damaging statements, such as saying that you could never accept your son, you could apologize by saying:

When I said that I could never accept you, it came out of a place of fear and not understanding what being gay means. I truly apologize for this. I do love you, and I do accept you. I hope I never make you doubt that again. I have been doing some reflection and some research, and I feel better equipped to have some honest discussions with you. I hope you will give me another chance to listen to you, because this time, it will be with an open and accepting mind and heart.

Grant Andrews & Malan van der Walt

Is my son really the same person? He seems so different to me.

Your son is undergoing a lot of changes in his life as he learns to accept himself. He might be making new friends, start dating or discover new interests. He might not even act exactly the same way he did when he was in the closet: he might dress differently or be less guarded about certain parts of his personality or mannerisms that he might have been hiding before for fear of being bullied or disliked.

In some senses, he is becoming a new person: one who accepts his identity. But in all other senses he is the same child that you raised and loved. He has the same values and the same heart. He has just decided to be authentic as he moves forward in life.

It is important to note that these changes might also bring challenges, and not all of the changes will be positive. For example, he might face more discrimination when he comes out of the closet, or even engage in some risky behaviors which you have learned about in the sections above. You also need to make sure that he is dealing with this process well emotionally, and he might need counselling if it becomes very hard for him. Both of the authors and many of the gay people we work with have shared how incredibly difficult the process of self-acceptance can be, and some of the changes you notice, if they impact his functioning, might be cause for concern.

While he might seem somewhat different than before, you should remember that this is his way of finding freedom and acceptance in his identity, and you are gaining access to parts of him that you never knew before. Try to cherish this process of discovery, and make sure he knows that you love him, support him and want the best for him.

How do I talk to my son about sex and the risk of HIV?

You will know from reading the previous sections that HIV is a real, serious threat for gay men. HIV, or the human immunodeficiency virus, is a virus affecting the immune system of humans. It can be contracted if the mouth, vagina, anus, tip of the penis or breaks in the skin (sores, burns or cuts, even small ones) are exposed to the bodily fluids of another person who already has the virus. These bodily fluids include semen, blood, vaginal fluids and breast milk. The risk of contracting HIV is highest for penetrative anal sex without a condom, and men or women who are the receptive partners in anal sex are at the greatest risk. HIV which is not closely monitored and treated will develop into AIDS, or acquired immune-deficiency syndrome, which is when the immune system is so weak that the body becomes susceptible to a host of *opportunistic infections,* and this often leads to death. There is currently no approved cure or vaccine for HIV, although there are treatments to prevent it from developing into AIDS and to ward off opportunistic infections.

However, if your son has safe, healthy sexual practices, which are aided by positive attitudes towards his own sexuality and to sex in general, then there is no reason to believe that he is more at risk for contracting HIV than the general population. These safe sexual practices include having only one sexual partner at a time, getting tested for HIV regularly, avoiding substances which could alter his judgment, and using condoms for all sexual encounters. Be aware that extremely oppressed environments usually lead to risky, unprotected sex, so we encourage you not to demonize sex for your son. If you would like to encourage your son to explore his sexuality in a healthy way, you can consider saying the following:

Your sexuality is a beautiful, wondrous, exciting part of yourself. It can lead you to a person one day that will add immeasurable value to your life: he will love you, cherish you, look out for your best interests at all times, and will be loyal and committed to you. That is what I want for you and that is what I know you deserve. So sex is a great adventure and can offer you wonderful rewards.

As noted, men who have sex with men are much more at risk of contracting HIV. As people working in the public health and public education sector, we feel that not enough safer sex messaging is targeted at MSM. If you would like to do the commendable thing of having this difficult conversation with your son, we would suggest that you add the following bit to your script:

But I want you to think about the fact that men who have sex with men are at greater risk for contracting sexually transmitted infections and HIV. We really want to encourage you to use a condom every time you have sex in order to protect your health. We also want to let you know that HIV has no cure, and, importantly, there are often no signs that your partner might have HIV. No matter how great he is, no matter how trustworthy you think he might be, none of these instincts can indicate to you whether or not he is HIV positive. You only need to have one unprotected sexual encounter with someone who is infected with HIV in order to be infected yourself, and the virus will be with you for life. Please protect yourself, get tested together before you sleep with him, and as far as possible keep sex for a long-term, loving, trusting relationship. We want you to enjoy sex, but not to allow it to become dangerous or destructive in your life. We can assure you that sex is more pleasurable and much safer when you really love and are committed to someone.

Grant Andrews & Malan van der Walt

I would like my son to abstain from sex. Should I tell him this?

There are a number of gay people who are abstaining from sex until marriage in accordance with either religious beliefs or personal preference (at least in places where gay marriage is legal). If it is your son's choice to abstain from sex, you can support him in this, but please be aware that trying to enforce abstinence on young people very rarely works and it would be a better idea to inform him about safe sex options even if you would prefer that he abstain. He will probably have sex anyway, as all of the best research shows that abstinence-only sex education does not decrease[82] the rate of sexual activity among students, and that over 70% of young people are or have been sexually active by the age of 19[83]. The research suggests that even when communities have very conservative attitudes towards sex, this does not cause more young people to abstain, but rather to engage in riskier or secretive behavior since they have negative attitudes towards sex. It is important for you and your son to know that secretive, guilt- and shame-ridden sexual behavior is strongly associated with HIV infection[84]: if you absorb the message that premarital sex is wrong and sinful, you might understand such messages to imply that you are worthy of scorn and judgment. Such self-beliefs lead you to devalue yourself, and decreases the likelihood that you value your health enough to practise safe sex.

If you want to encourage your child to talk to you about his life and not hide his sexual desires or experiences, or possibly to engage in even riskier behaviors, the only way to do this is to have open communication and not try to enforce restrictions on him which he does not agree to.

I'm worried about what people will say about my son or about me.

If you are based in a community that is socially conservative, it is to be expected that you are concerned about how you will be treated by members of this community. People who are likely to spout off homophobic rhetoric are unlikely to have encountered openly gay people, and therefore homosexuality hasn't become 'normalized' for them. This could be based on their untested assumptions about gay men, likely their highly specific and selective focus on certain Biblical verses, and possibly a simple tendency towards somewhat bigoted behavior.

Instead of seeing this as a threat to you and your child, you can consider this to be an important opportunity to normalize homosexuality for your son by being openly accepting and loving of him. What is often neglected by gay self-help literature, is the journey that the parents and family of gay people undertake. It is not just your son that comes out of the closet, but you and your family have a coming out process as the parents and relatives of a gay man. You may find this challenging and even anxiety-inducing. In some situations you might still avoid talking about your son being gay. Do not blame yourself for your reactions needlessly. Accept that this is your reality.

How can I help combat homophobia in my community?

We would like to point out to you that you have been presented with an opportunity to help change people's mindsets, step by step and person by person. One of the most effective and non-demanding ways to accomplish this is to merely continue with your life the same way as you have before. Do not hide away in your home, do not avoid contact with your son, do not do anything that might fuel negative sentiment against gay people. Instead, show people that having a gay son is a normal part of your life by not changing your behavior or conduct with your son.

How to Understand and Accept Your Gay Son

If you have a bit of an advocate bent, and would like to lend your voice to the choir of gay people and their families who advocate for the human rights of LGBT people, find out what your local laws are. If there are any anti-gay or anti-LGBT laws in place, phone or mail your local government and demand change. Your vote is your power. You will feel better by taking the opportunity to demonstrate your acceptance and support of your gay son.

By now, it is likely that you have gained greater sensitivity for the plight of gay men, especially as they deal with homophobia. It is also likely that you might encounter expressions or demonstrations of homophobia yourself. You might feel anger at such instances of injustice, and feel compelled to take some sort of action. Perhaps you might even be tempted to take retributive action, and react in kind, which would be a place of hatred and fear. Resist this temptation. Rather, see it as an opportunity to spread awareness, to be kind in the face of intolerance. Should you encounter a person referring to gay men in a homophobic way, you can consider using the idea of what to say which was given earlier in this section in confronting homophobia:

What you have just said is homophobic. It is probably based on not having met gay people before (at least that you're aware of), or relying on outdated ideas of what it means to be gay, and whether it is right or wrong. However, I want you to know that your homophobia is damaging and offensive, and I would like you to reconsider before you say things that are hurtful and damning to people who do not deserve such treatment. Thank you for listening to me.

It is better not to belabour your points: through this script, you are succinctly identifying the behavior of this person, offering understanding of why they are behaving in such a way, but, importantly, pointing out that such behavior is not acceptable. This is not always easy to do, but a nonconfrontational, gentle approach is much more likely to be effective than an approach sullied by anger and a need for retribution. Often the very fact that someone is standing up to bigotry and heterosexism is enough to give your son and other young teens the courage to stand up for themselves about their sexual identities.

What if my partner or co-parent does not accept my son, but I do?

This is ultimately a distressing situation, for both you and your partner. However, the fact that you are at a place of acceptance should demonstrate to you that even when it feels very hard to accept that your son is gay, it is possible. This means that the same can happen for your partner.

How to Understand and Accept Your Gay Son

While it might be hard, try to be understanding of their process as well, and do not apply too much pressure on them to come to terms with your son's sexuality overnight. We suggest that you might say something like the following to your son:

As you know, _____ has not yet come to terms with your sexuality. It is disappointing to me, as I am sure it is disappointing to you. You might remember that it took some work on my part to reach the space I am in currently, and we can hope together that the same will be true for _____. Throughout this, I will stand by you and support you.

You might also want to have an honest, calm conversation with your partner to discover the reasons why they are finding it so hard to accept your son. Don't try to antagonise them in this process, but again remember that it took you a while to accept your son as well. Perhaps you can point them to information in this book or from the resources we provide in order to aid their process of coming to terms with your son being gay.

I won't have any grandchildren. This makes me really sad and disappointed.

It is normal and to be expected that you might be mournful about the fact that your son will not have a traditional nuclear family. However, it would be a mistake to automatically assume that you will not be a proud grandparent one day. While different in some respects, your son may still become a father one day via adoption or surrogacy. It might be different to the way that you once expected, but you will still be experiencing all of the joys of being a grandparent. And it is no secret that families with adopted children are just as likely to thrive as families with biological children.

Also remember that your son is affected by the biological realities of gay parenthood as well. The struggle to have a child might be a hardship in his life as well.

We recommend that you revise your original mindset when it comes to grandchildren: is your need for (biological) grandchildren coming from the desire to see your own son truly be happy and fulfilled, or is it due to your own needs? We are not trying to say that having a desire to be a grandparent is a bad thing, but we think it is important to be mindful of the fact that your son's inclination to have children is a decision that is entirely up to him. Remember too that an increasing number of heterosexual couples are choosing not to have children and therefore more and more parents are having to start thinking differently about grandchildren.

I feel more settled in my new identity as the parent of a gay son. But I am not sure how to tell important people in my life about this.

It might have been very difficult for you to reach this point. This journey is a difficult one to embark on for many people, but it has many rewards for you and your son.

It is important to assess how far you have come in coming to terms with your son's sexuality. If you are not in a place of complete acceptance and peace, those you share this news with might sense this and respond in kind.

It is entirely possible that some of these important people in your life have already observed that your son might be gay. If that is the case, then the news will not come as a shock to them. However, this does not necessarily mean that they will definitely be open and welcoming to this information. We recommend that you prepare yourself for this possibility.

The person that is most affected by having his sexual orientation revealed to his family, is your son. Therefore, it is important that you approach your son and ask him how he would feel if his sexual orientation becomes known to others. You know your son better than anyone, so you should be able to gauge from his reaction if he is ready for those close to him to know this information. Perhaps he won't be ready when you expect him to be, or perhaps he won't be ready even if you feel ready. Honor his wishes and work on a timeline that makes sense for him.

Once that important moment has arrived, and he shares his willingness to let the family know, ask him if he would like you to speak on his behalf, or if he would like to share this news by himself. If he wants to say the words himself, we would recommend that you commend him on his bravery, and then present him with a few pointers:

I admire your bravery in wanting to tell our family directly. Before we make plans to tell everybody, I would just like to remind you that the news you are sharing might shock and even upset some people. So I think the best way to handle this is with sensitivity. Be true to yourself, but also understand the process that our family might have to go through to truly come to terms with it. Above all, I want you to remember that I am your number one supporter, that I am very proud of you, and that I love every part of who you are.

Should your son not be willing to disclose his sexuality to family and family friends, but rather leave it to your discretion, here are some ideas on how you can relay this information:

A while ago, my son shared some important news with me, and now I would like to share it with you. Before I do, I would like you to bear in mind that this is an important part of his identity, that we love him no less for it, and that we accept him unconditionally. While it might take you some time to get used to this, we expect you to treat him no differently, and to love him no less. Our son is gay.

Are there any additional resources which I can use to aid me in my journey of accepting my gay son?

Fortunately, as we live in the digital age, the resources to aid you in understanding and accepting your gay son are plentiful. For your convenience, we have arranged some of these resources under separate headings, to hopefully meet your specific needs.

Advocacy groups and informational sites

An extensive list of resources can be found at the Ithaca College Center for LGBT Education, Outreach and Services website, including academic, advocacy and health sites. You can browse through the resources at http://www.ithaca.edu/sacl/lgbt/resources/other/[85]

Two of the most prominent advocacy groups are GLAAD and the HRC. Both sites provide news and information about LGBT concerns:

GLAAD: http://www.glaad.org/[86] The Gay and Lesbian Alliance Against Defamation.

HRC: http://www.hrc.org/[87] Human Rights Campaign.

The official PFLAG site has a host of informational and support resources. You can even find a PFLAG chapter near you on their website, or find hotlines and other resources to answer your questions. There are over 500 PFLAG chapters in the US alone, as well as many international chapters. PFLAG really provides a comprehensive list of resources for all of the questions raised in this book as well as many others you might still have, so we highly recommend visiting their site. You can talk to other parents who are in the same position as you are, and hear how they dealt with the struggles you are going through: http://community.pflag.org/[88]

Representations of Gay Men

Many parents want to understand their gay sons better and might struggle to communicate with them effectively when they first come out. These films and television shows could give you some insight into what your son is going through.

Bridegroom: A Love Story, Unequaled (Documentary directed by Linda Bloodworth-Thomason)

This film shares the heartbreaking true love story of Shane Bitney Crone and his late partner, Thomas Lee Bridegroom. Their powerful love was cut short by Bridegrooms death in a tragic accident, and Crone was denied from attending the funeral of his partner of six years. The documentary touches on homophobia and family acceptance, but ultimately is about the love that was shared between Crone and Bridegroom.

Brokeback Mountain (Directed by Ang Lee)

The seminal gay-themed film, *Brokeback Mountain* is a romantic drama that tells the heartbreaking story of a ranch hand and a rodeo cowboy who fall in love in the early 1960s. While sombre in tone, this movie does a brilliant job in portraying the damaging effects of a homophobic, unaccepting society, and how this can lead to devastating consequences.

Homosexuality and Religion

For the Bible Tells Me So (Directed by Daniel G. Karslake), is a critically acclaimed documentary that offers a comprehensive look at how Bible verses discussing homosexuality have been interpreted in modern times. In addition to religious scholars offering an explanation of why the Bible seems to condemn homosexuality at first glance, it also traces the stories of five families that have a gay son or lesbian daughter.

Prayers for Bobby (Directed by Russell Mulcahy) is a film that resonates with many religious families who have a gay son. Based on true events, this critical favourite tells the story of a conservative and deeply religious mother who cannot come to terms with her teenage son's homosexuality, to devastating consequences.

Romantic Drama

Shelter (Directed by Jonah Markowitz). A sweet, unassuming romantic drama, *Shelter* tells the story of two surfers who find love despite obstacles presented by their families. Not as angst-filled as many other gay-themed movies, you can appreciate this movie for sensitising you towards gay relationships, and you can appreciate the smooth, slow burn story progression as it mirrors real life.

How to Understand and Accept Your Gay Son

Other notable titles are *Yossi and Jagger*, *A Single Man*, and *The Object of My Affection*.

Coming Out Stories

A soldier coming out to his father:
https://www.youtube.com/watch?v=DVAgz6iyK6A[89]

Troye Sivan shares his coming out story
https://www.youtube.com/watch?v=JoL-MnXvK80[90]

Connor Franta coming out to his YouTube fans:
https://www.youtube.com/watch?v=WYodBfRxKWI[91]

A teenager named Vincent shares his story on the Tyra Banks Show after being forced to undergo an exorcism in order to try and cure his homosexuality.
https://www.youtube.com/watch?v=wXcWygr8vEM[92]

Another YouTube clip[93] focuses on twin brothers coming out to their father, and shows their emotional and heart-rending coming out process.

Grant Andrews & Malan van der Walt

Television Shows

An important television moment was Ellen DeGeneres coming out in her sitcom television show in 1997 in the episode entitled "The Puppy Episode". It offers a great dramatization of what the coming out process is like, and can be easily found online.

Television shows with dynamic representations of gay people and same-sex couples include *Empire, Modern Family, Brooklyn Nine-Nine, Grey's Anatomy, Glee, Happy Endings, Will & Grace, Six Feet Under, United States of Tara, General Hospital, The Office* and *Desperate Housewives*.

Gay History/ Gay Rights

The Normal Heart (Directed by Ryan Murphy) tells the story of the AIDS crisis in New York in the 1980s.

Milk (directed by Gus Van Sant) tells the story of Harvey Milk, the first openly gay man elected to notable public office in the US.

The Celluloid Closet (Directed by Jeffrey Friedman and Rob Epstein) is a documentary showing the history of representations of LGBT people in cinema.

How to Understand and Accept Your Gay Son

Stonewall Uprising (Directed by Kate Davis and David Heilbroner) is a documentary depicting the 1969 Stonewall riots.

Books worth reading

PFLAG NYC has created a great list of reading material for parents of LGBTQI children. These range from informational books to personal stories. You can find their list and links to the books at http://www.pflagnyc.org/support/suggestedreading[94]

Glossary

Gender noncomforming: This is any behaviour or gender expression which does not match the gender roles which society has set for men and women.

Heterosexism: The system of attitudes, bias and discrimination which favors heterosexuality, such as thinking that straight relationships are superior or assuming that everyone you meet is straight.

Heterosocial relationships: Friendships or platonic relationships with people of the opposite sex.

Internalized homophobia: Negative feelings which gay people have towards themselves or other gay people.

Learned helplessness: A state of believing that there is nothing one can do to improve a certain situation.

Minority stress: The chronically high levels of stress faced by people who are part of minority groups.

MSM: Men who have sex with men. These do not only include gay men, but also those who identify as straight, bisexual, or who choose not to identify under these labels, but who have sex with men.

Opportunistic infections: For those infected with HIV or AIDS, these are infections which take advantage of the fact that the body has a lowered immune system. They do not usually infect those with healthy immune systems.

Pathologize: To think of something as psychologically abnormal, or to treat it as such.

Straight/ heterosexual privilege: These are benefits which are given to those who are straight or perceived to be straight, but denied to those who are LGBT. This includes things like being given immediate access to loved ones in case of an emergency, being able to show public displays of affection without fear of homophobia, and being able to regularly see relationships which mirror yours in media.

Suicidal ideation: Thoughts about suicide or planning how to take one's own life.

Grant Andrews & Malan van der Walt

About the authors

Grant Andrews is currently completing his PhD at the University of the Western Cape, with a focus on fatherhood and masculinities. He lectures in the English Department and has written extensively on self-actualization and self-exploration in his previous book "The Joy of Being Incomplete". His professional focus is on leadership projects and capacity building.

Malan van der Walt is a student program coordinator at the University of Stellenbosch, working with young lesbian, gay, bisexual and transgender people in order to promote HIV prevention and to advocate for equality. He is continuing his postgraduate studies in psychology with a focus on gender and sexuality. He conducts counselling sessions and runs support groups with young gay people.

They live together with their two dogs, Billy and Coby, in Cape Town, South Africa.

If you enjoyed this book or found it useful we would be very grateful if you would post a short review on Amazon. Your support really does make a difference and we read all the reviews personally so we can get your feedback and make this book even better.

Find out more at http://www.inspiredlivingbooks.com

References

[1] http://www.huffingtonpost.com/2015/01/11/straight-guys-holding-hands-homophobia_n_6446684.html

[2] http://www.economist.com/news/middle-east-and-africa/21597943-diplomatic-pressure-did-not-stop-absurd-law-deadly-intolerance

[3] https://books.google.co.za/books?id=dRJLGKgjS3oC&printsec=frontcover&dq=isbn:0226034011&hl=en&sa=X&ei=sbrQVKjzCov1Ututg7gC&ved=0CB0Q6AEwAA

[4] http://www.kinseyinstitute.org/research/ak-hhscale.html

[5] http://books.google.co.za/books/about/Sexual_Behavior_in_the_Human_Male.html?id=pfMKrY3VvigC&redir_esc=y

[6] http://en.wikipedia.org/wiki/Effeminacy

[7] http://pediatrics.aappublications.org/content/113/6/1827.long

[8] http://web.archive.org/web/20130808032050/http://www.apa.org/helpcenter/sexual-orientation.aspx

[9] http://www.crosswalk.com/blogs/dr-warren-throckmorton/does-father-absence-cause-homosexuality-11596147.html

[10] http://www.apa.org/topics/lgbt/orientation.aspx

[11] http://psychology.ucdavis.edu/faculty_sites/rainbow/html/facts_changing.html

[12] https://gactupdate.wordpress.com/notes/suicide/

[13] http://www.ibtimes.co.uk/alan-chambers-gay-cure-conversion-therapy-closes-481981

[14] http://76crimes.com/ex-gay-therapy-what-reputable-experts-have-to-say/

[15] http://en.wikipedia.org/wiki/Ex-gay_movement

[16] http://en.wikipedia.org/wiki/Conversion_therapy

[17] http://www.theguardian.com/science/brain-flapping/2015/jan/08/homosexuality-gay-choice-psychology

[18] http://www.theguardian.com/science/2014/feb/14/genes-influence-male-sexual-orientation-study

[19] http://www.newscientist.com/article/dn26572-largest-study-of-gay-brothers-homes-in-on-gay-genes.html

[20] http://en.wikipedia.org/wiki/Biology_and_sexual_orientation

21

http://www.telegraph.co.uk/news/worldnews/europe/italy/1474047/Homosexual-link-to-fertility-genes.html

[22] http://www.sciencedirect.com/science/article/pii/S0018506X01916812

[23] http://www.advocate.com/health/2012/08/06/new-theory-says-sexual-orientation-determined-brain-hemisphere-dominance

[24] http://motherboard.vice.com/read/more-evidence-sexuality-is-innate-gay-men-respond-to-male-sex-pheromones

[25] http://www.thetrevorproject.org/pages/facts-about-suicide

26

http://www.violencepreventionworks.org/public/bullying_sexual_orientation.page

[27] http://www.ncbi.nlm.nih.gov/pmc/articles/PMC2072932/

[28] http://www.bbc.com/news/world-africa-29994678

29

http://www.washingtonpost.com/blogs/worldviews/wp/2014/02/24/here-are-the-10-countries-where-homosexuality-may-be-punished-by-death/

[30] http://mg.co.za/article/2014-04-11-men-are-also-corrective-rape-victims

[31] http://magazine.good.is/articles/gay-sex-is-not-anal-sex

[32] http://kinseyconfidential.org/common-anal-sex-heterosexual-couples/

[33] http://www.huffingtonpost.com/2012/01/06/anal-sex-heterosexual-couples-report_n_1190440.html

[34] http://www.cosmopolitan.com/sex-love/news/a17749/anal-sex-misconceptions/

[35] http://www.transequality.org/PDFs/US Civ Rts Commn NCTE statement 5 6 11.pdf

[36] http://www.iwpr.org/initiatives/pay-equity-and-discrimination

[37] http://broadblogs.com/2011/03/30/it%E2%80%99s-ok-to-be-a-tomboy-but-not-a-sissy-why/

[38] http://www.gsanetwork.org/files/aboutus/GSA_GNC_FINAL-web.pdf

[39] http://www.theguardian.com/commentisfree/2010/oct/19/gay-men-promiscuous-myth

[40] http://www.aidsmap.com/Consistent-decline-in-partner-numbers-in-US-gay-men-in-last-decade-but-no-change-in-condom-use/page/2635086/

41

https://www.google.co.za/url?sa=t&rct=j&q=&esrc=s&source=web&cd=1&cad=rja&uact=8&ved=0CBwQFjAA&url=http%3A%2F%2Fwww.aidsmap.com%2FHIV-transmission-risk-during-anal-sex-18-times-higher-

than-during-vaginal-sex%2Fpage%2F1446187%2F&ei=DerQVP39EYHBUpCxgNAJ&usg=AFQjCNFpTlJ7yLP6V_DjVd4FvZhntTtfWA&sig2=qewITM78wq2_z6nJMF6Dnw&bvm=bv.85076809,d.ZGU
[42] https://www.aids.gov/hiv-aids-basics/hiv-aids-101/statistics/
[43] http://www.cdc.gov/hiv/risk/gender/msm/facts/
[44] http://www.avert.org/worldwide-hiv-aids-statistics.htm
[45] http://www.imdb.com/title/tt0912583/
[46] http://www.amazon.com/God-Gay-Christian-Biblical-Relationships/dp/1601425163
[47] http://www.amazon.com/What-Bible-Really-About-Homosexuality-ebook/dp/B005BTQEQ4
[48] http://www.amazon.com/Bibles-Yes-Same-Sex-Marriage-Evangelicals-ebook/dp/B00LAAB6IY
[49] https://www.youtube.com/watch?v=gmp6lLct-fQ
[50] http://en.wikipedia.org/wiki/The_Bible_and_homosexuality
[51] http://www.gaychristian101.com/
[52] http://www.religioustolerance.org/
[53] http://www.salon.com/2012/01/22/the_invention_of_the_heterosexual/
[54] http://gaylife.about.com/od/comingout/a/population.htm
[55] http://en.wikipedia.org/wiki/Societal_attitudes_toward_homosexuality
[56] http://books.google.co.za/books/about/Patterns_of_sexual_behavior.html?id=cjQEAQAAIAAJ&redir_esc=y
[57] http://www.huffingtonpost.com/2014/10/19/pope-homosexuality-church-gay_n_6010904.html
[58] http://en.wikipedia.org/wiki/Gene_Robinson
[59] http://www.globalequality.org/component/content/article/166
[60] http://www.queerculturalcenter.org/Pages/Keehnen/Siegel.html
[61] http://en.wikipedia.org/wiki/Counterculture
[62] http://en.wikipedia.org/wiki/Drag_queen
[63] http://thinkprogress.org/lgbt/2012/07/12/515641/study-40-percent-of-homeless-youth-are-lgbt-family-rejection-is-leading-cause/
[64] http://www.eurad.net/en/news/consumption_data/New+study%3A+Drugs+and+the+Gay+community.9UFRnMXr.ips
[65] http://www.independent.co.uk/life-style/health-and-families/health-news/drug-use-seven-times-higher-among-gays-8165971.html

[66] http://www.jhsph.edu/research/centers-and-institutes/center-for-adolescent-health/research/_includes/MARS_Report.pdf
[67] http://www.muirwoodteen.com/teen-drug-addiction/who-is-at-risk/
[68] http://www.apa.org/news/press/releases/2008/01/satisfaction.aspx
[69] http://www.pewsocialtrends.org/2013/06/13/a-survey-of-lgbt-americans/
[70] http://abcnews.go.com/2020/story?id=124123
[71] http://www.apa.org/monitor/2010/10/same-sex.aspx
[72] http://www.theguardian.com/society/2011/sep/11/gay-people-risk-old-age
[73] http://www.advocate.com/politics/marriage-equality/2014/12/13/report-same-sex-couples-less-likely-divorce
[74] http://www.boxturtlebulletin.com/Articles/000,002.htm
[75] http://www.yalescientific.org/2012/03/do-animals-exhibit-homosexuality/
[76] http://mic.com/articles/83281/what-the-research-really-says-about-gay-parents-and-kids
[77] http://mic.com/articles/92945/a-major-study-reveals-what-happens-to-children-raised-by-same-sex-couples
[78] http://www.advocate.com/health/ask-doctor/2010/09/15/depression-and-anxiety
[79] http://www.amazon.com/Tango-Makes-Three-Justin-Richardson-ebook/dp/B007QXVHJW/ref=sr_1_2?ie=UTF8&qid=1418218561&sr=8-2&keywords=children%27s+books+gay
[80] http://www.demilked.com/gay-couples-lgbt-all-love-is-equal-braden-summers/
[81] http://www.huffingtonpost.com/2013/06/20/michael-bussee-exodus-international-ex-gay_n_3475243.html
[82] http://www.advocatesforyouth.org/publications/publications-a-z/409-the-truth-about-abstinence-only-programs
[83] https://www.dosomething.org/facts/11-facts-about-sexual-health-teens-us
[84] http://www.advocatesforyouth.org/publications/publications-a-z/524-understanding-disparities-in-the-hiv-epidemic-
[85] http://www.ithaca.edu/sacl/lgbt/resources/other/
[86] http://www.glaad.org/
[87] http://www.hrc.org/
[88] http://community.pflag.org/
[89] https://www.youtube.com/watch?v=DVAgz6iyK6A
[90] https://www.youtube.com/watch?v=JoL-MnXvK80

[91] https://www.youtube.com/watch?v=WYodBfRxKWI
[92] https://www.youtube.com/watch?v=wXcWygr8vEM
[93] https://www.youtube.com/watch?v=L3K0CJ8usPU
[94] http://www.pflagnyc.org/support/suggestedreading

Printed in Great Britain
by Amazon